A Dance of Polar Opposites

Eastman Studies in Music

Ralph P. Locke, Senior Editor
Eastman School of Music

Additional Titles of Interest

CageTalk:
Dialogues with and about John Cage
Edited by Peter Dickinson

Concert Music, Rock, and Jazz since 1945:
Essays and Analytic Studies
Edited by Richard Hermann and
Elizabeth West Marvin

Elliott Carter:
Collected Essays and Lectures, 1937–1995
Edited by Jonathan W. Bernard

György Kurtág:
Three Interviews and Ligeti Homages
Compiled and Edited by
Bálint András Varga

Intimate Voices:
The Twentieth-Century String Quartet
Edited by Evan Jones

Leon Kirchner:
Composer, Performer, and Teacher
Robert Riggs

Music of Luigi Dallapiccola
Raymond Fearn

Othmar Schoeck: Life and Works
Chris Walton

The Pleasure of Modernist Music:
Listening, Meaning, Intention, Ideology
Edited by Arved Ashby

Samuel Barber Remembered:
A Centenary Tribute
Peter Dickinson

The Sea on Fire: Jean Barraqué
Paul Griffiths

Three Questions for Sixty-Five Composers
Bálint András Varga

The Whistling Blackbird:
Essays and Talks on New Music
Robert Morris

A complete list of titles in the Eastman Studies in Music series may be found on the University of Rochester Press website, www.urpress.com.

A Dance of
Polar Opposites

The Continuing Transformation of
Our Musical Language

George Rochberg

Edited with an Introduction by Jeremy Gill

R. UNIVERSITY OF ROCHESTER PRESS

First published 2012

University of Rochester Press
668 Mt. Hope Avenue, Rochester, NY 14620, USA
www.urpress.com
and Boydell & Brewer Limited
PO Box 9, Woodbridge, Suffolk IP12 3DF, UK
www.boydellandbrewer.com

ISBN-13: 978-1-58046-413-0
ISSN: 1071-9989

Library of Congress Cataloging-in-Publication Data

Rochberg, George.
   A dance of polar opposites : the continuing transformation of our musical
language / George Rochberg ; edited with an introduction by Jeremy Gill.
      pages cm. — (Eastman studies in music, ISSN 1071-9989 ; v. 88)
   Includes bibliographical references and index.
   ISBN 978-1-58046-413-0 (hardcover : alk. paper) 1. Music theory. 2. Musical analysis.
3. Tonality. I. Gill, Jeremy, editor. II. Title. III. Series: Eastman studies in music ; v. 88.
   MT6.R763   2012
   781—dc23
                                                2012006782

A catalogue record for this title is available from the British Library.

This publication is printed on acid-free paper.
Printed in the United States of America.

We are not slaves of history, we can
choose and create our own time.
—George Rochberg

Contents

Acknowledgments

I would like to thank Sudha Arunachalam, Richard Griscom, Michael Klein, Misti Shaw, and Greg Wilder for their careful reading of the first draft of *A Dance of Polar Opposites*. As I condensed Rochberg's nearly one-thousand-page manuscript to its current size, it was essential that the thread of his argument and the essence of his work be maintained. Their probing questions and insightful comments were invaluable. Highest praise and thanks are due Karen E. Wolfgang-Swanson for her broad knowledge that contributed greatly to her superb copyediting. Thanks, as well, to Dr. Lenora D. Wolfgang for her close reading of the text and her excellent suggestions.

Additionally, I thank Boosey & Hawkes, Carl Fischer, G. Schirmer & Associated Music Publishers, Hal Leonard Corporation, and Schott Music Corporation for permission to reprint copyrighted music. And for permission to reprint copyrighted texts, I thank Princeton University Press, Simon & Schuster, and Wesleyan University Press.

Above all, I thank Gene Rochberg, who chose me to make this edited version of her husband's manuscript, and who singlehandedly made its completion possible. Her dedication to this project, and to seeing all the work of her husband preserved and made available, is an inspiration.

JG

Introduction

Jeremy Gill

In 1955 George Rochberg published *The Hexachord and Its Relation to the 12-Tone Row*, an inquiry into the later music of Arnold Schoenberg that Rochberg wrote "out of a need to clarify problems which concerned [him] as a composer."[1] Although he temporarily adopted the method for his own musical language, Rochberg was wary of twelve-tone composition: it ran the risk of falling into what he called the "indefensible practice" of "arbitrarily throwing together abstract conglomerates of pitches," as opposed to the "genuinely heard harmony" of tonal practice.[2] Schoenberg's "invertible" hexachord, however, with its combinatorial capacities and foundational symmetrical structure, provided limited, therefore predictable, and above all audibly consistent chordal structures, and was at the heart of Rochberg's own developing twelve-tone language.

When he began teaching at the University of Pennsylvania in 1961, Rochberg turned his theoretical attention to the great works of the nineteenth century. Hitherto preoccupied with combinatoriality in particular and symmetrical thinking in general, he was drawn to the instances of symmetrical construction he discovered in these works, still primarily governed by the asymmetrical tonal system. Two years later, he wrote his last exclusively twelve-tone work (his First Piano Trio) and between 1965 and 1972 wrote a series of works, beginning with *Contra mortem et tempus* and *Music for the Magic Theater* and culminating in the Third String Quartet, which used a new musical language based on connections and juxtapositions between asymmetrical tonality and symmetrical atonality.

He found these connections—common ground between the tonal and atonal worlds—in the later works of Schoenberg and his pupil Webern, where tonal functions seemed to be returning through the back door of symmetrically derived harmonies. He began collecting his theoretical findings in what eventually became a massive work called *Chromaticism*,[3] still in progress at his death in 2005, although as early as 1993 he anticipated its conclusion in a letter to his Canadian friend and fellow composer Istvan Anhalt.[4] In 1995 he extracted from it material for an essay titled "Polarity in Music: Symmetry, Asymmetry, and Their Consequences" (included in the 2004 edition of *The Aesthetics of Survival*), which, incidentally, provides a fine introduction to the present book's ideas.

Chromaticism, here substantially revised and renamed *A Dance of Polar Opposites,* began with *The Hexachord and Its Relation to the 12-Tone Row* and included two other contemporaneous extended explorations of hexachordal combinatoriality and its ramifications. These were followed by copious writings on the incursion of symmetry into the asymmetrical tonal world of the late eighteenth and nineteenth centuries, including an idiosyncratic review of diatonic harmony, explaining his discovery of what he called "circular harmonic sets," and formulating new ways to conceive of large-scale pitch organization, both tonal and posttonal. Following these sections were essays on late Webern and polarity in music, and a handful of philosophical speculations on poets, composers, and even one on the theorist Donald Francis Tovey, whose work Rochberg discovered in 1944. Rochberg's manuscript ended with an affirmation of dualities—a "dance of polar opposites"[5]—and advocated the juxtaposition of perceivable styles and languages rather than a cohesive language based on their union.

In preparing *A Dance of Polar Opposites,* I have retained the basic layout of *Chromaticism,* but deleted the opening sections on hexachords and twelve-tone theory as these were mostly published in Rochberg's lifetime[6] (only an exhaustive account of the properties of the Hauer tropes remains unpublished, but it has little value without this context). I have divided Rochberg's writings on tonal music, which formed the centerpiece of the manuscript, into three parts.

Part 1, "Setting the Stage," begins with a chapter on "The Morphology of Musical Language," describing how (and why) musical language continually transforms itself. Chapter 2 continues with the most relevant parts of Rochberg's review of tonal harmony. Of particular interest is his description of the Neapolitan (tone), drawn down to the tonic (rather than to the leading-tone, as in traditional voice-leading), as an equal, balancing tendency to that of the leading-tone. These double leading-tones, combined, result in the "altered" chords, or augmented sixths (Italian, French, German), that Rochberg thought of as intensified dominants, and that could just as easily resolve to I as to V. This way of thinking becomes particularly important when reading his analysis of the first variation from Webern's Opus 30 in chapter 9. Chapter 2 ends with a discussion of the ambiguities of enharmonic spelling and the bi-, tri-, and tetradirectional progressions that result from those ambiguities.

Part 2, "Symmetry in Tonal Music," lays out—in three distinct stages— the incursion of symmetry into asymmetrical tonal music. Chapter 3 presents embryonic circular sets—all incomplete—that include one example each of the multidirectional possibilities presented in part 1: governed by the tritone (in an example from Mozart), the major third (Beethoven), and the minor third (Schubert). Chapter 4 gives examples of more evolved sets. These are complete circular sets, possessing all their constituent members, but only locally functional. Finally, chapter 5 presents fully evolved circular sets as those that both are complete and govern whole works (as in the example from Chopin) or large sections of works (Brahms and Tchaikovsky). Fully evolved circular sets, as symmetrically derived, necessarily dethrone the dominant and pave the way to posttonal processes.

Part 3, "Pitch Organization on Larger Scales," mixes the tonal and atonal in a complex of terms Rochberg coined in his attempts to describe large-scale pitch organization. In direct contrast to serial analysis, which tends toward the microscopic, he sought ways to describe *heard* structures in music that had moved or were moving away from diatonic functionality. The *harmonic envelope* can be understood as a prolongation of a single harmony in tonal music, but prolonged to the point where its directional function evaporates, and it becomes an autonomous musical event or *locus*. The *harmonic field*, by contrast, is not so restricted, as it features a limited set of pitches that act as the materials from which a work or section of a work may be constructed. In the harmonic field, discrete harmonies change while the source of those harmonies remains unchanged. The *tonal field*, finally, is pure macro-structure, in which keys (or harmonic fields, possibly even harmonic envelopes) are arranged in a symmetrical fashion. Even in tonal works featuring tonal field construction the dominant is repressed, functioning in local contexts but never as a determining element in large-scale form.

In "Looking Ahead," part 4 of *A Dance of Polar Opposites*, I have combined the sections of *Chromaticism* dealing with Webern and polarity. That this section begins, paradoxically, with a look backward, reviewing Webern's entire career, is no accident. For Rochberg, the key to the future always lay in the past, even if sometimes buried. In the final chapter, "A New Circle of Fifths," he presents a full discussion of polar opposites, and in the Afterword continues the discussion in a broader sense, focusing on the poets Blake, Coleridge, and Yeats.

Rochberg's comment in his introduction to *The Hexachord and Its Relation to the 12-Tone Row*—that it was written to answer his concerns as a composer—applies equally well to the present book: it is useful to keep in mind that it is the work of a composer, not a theorist. Nevertheless, it is interesting to consider this work in a larger theoretical context, as many of Rochberg's ideas have been addressed by other writers.

Of the many composer-theorists of the twentieth century, George Perle is one who parallels Rochberg in many ways. Both originally from small cities in New Jersey, and nearly exact contemporaries (Perle was Rochberg's senior by three years and survived him by four), they immersed themselves in atonal and twelve-tone worlds early in their careers and each knew the other's theoretical work (Perle reviewed Rochberg's *Hexachord and Its Relation to the 12-Tone Row*, while Rochberg reviewed Perle's *Serial Composition and Atonality*).[7] Both were obsessed with symmetry in music, and both developed an approach to composition that melded the tonal and atonal. Later in life, both wrote less technical books for a wider musical audience (Rochberg's *The Aesthetics of Survival* appeared in 1984, Perle's *The Listening Composer* in 1990).

While there is no evidence that Rochberg was familiar with it, the work of Neo-Riemannian theorists parallels his attempts to understand specifically harmonic motions in tonal landscapes that feature weakened (or avoided) dominant-tonic relationships, supplanting them with root motions by major and minor thirds, the governing intervals of Rochberg's circular harmonic sets. Richard Cohn's "Introduction to Neo-Riemannian Theory" provides the historical background for Neo-Riemannian thought which, interestingly, includes a reference to Donald Francis Tovey,[8] whose work Rochberg did know. It is important to point out with regard to David Lewin (according to Cohn, the originator of Neo-Riemannian theory), that the term *Klang*, used by Riemann and Lewin to mean a consonant triad, means something very different for Rochberg. He defines it thoroughly in chapter 7 of the present volume, and it is sufficient here only to note the distinction.

Music theorists may find it surprising that Rochberg was apparently unaware of the burgeoning scholarly literature that traces symmetrically derived harmonies, progressions, and large-scale harmonic motions, particularly in Russian music. Much has been written—during the years when Rochberg was figuring these matters out on his own and in the years since his death—about symmetrical scales and chords in Rimsky-Korsakov, Scriabin, and Stravinsky, in particular, and an awareness of symmetrical procedures in the music of Wolf, Brahms, Schubert, and even Beethoven can be found today in undergraduate theory courses (Steven Laitz's textbook *The Complete Musician*, for example, devotes its last three chapters to symmetry in tonal music). Yet, in a footnote in *Chromaticism*,[9] Rochberg states that only in 1994 was he made aware of the presence of another theorist who studied symmetry's transformational action on tonality while he was presenting a paper on symmetrical chromatic harmony at Dartmouth College. Rochberg took great delight in Richard Taruskin's article, referred to him by one of his audience there (it is reprinted as chapter 4 in Taruskin's monumental *Stravinsky and the Russian Traditions*). In Taruskin, Rochberg found an analytic ally (both cite the same passage from Schubert's Ninth Symphony as a foreshadowing of Stravinsky's developing harmonic language, for example),[10] as well as a justification of his own theoretical work.

Throughout the long process of writing *Chromaticism*, Rochberg was, above all, finding in the music of the past what was useful to him as a composer, and, as he makes clear at the end of chapter 10 of the present volume, he was interested in communicating his insights, primarily, to other composers. Consequently, *A Dance of Polar Opposites* will be of particular interest to composers, providing a model of how one masterful composer came to understand his predecessors. Rochberg's analyses of his own music—*Serenata d'estate, Ricordanza, Sonata-Aria*—will interest students, performers, and admirers of his music. Theorists will most likely find this book to be of historical value, since many of its major themes are by now well understood. But Rochberg's approach to them is unique, and merits careful reading. Most important, this book—together with the recently published *Five Lines, Four Spaces* (Rochberg's memoirs) and *Eagle Minds* (letters between him and Istvan Anhalt)—paints a portrait of an artist of tremendous variety, insight, seriousness of purpose, and dedication to his craft.

Part One

Setting the Stage

Chapter One

The Morphology of Musical Language

In order to understand how musical language transforms itself slowly, over time, in what follows I trace the story of the emergence of symmetrical chromaticism from its asymmetrical tonal sources. Chiefly, I am guided by a biological analogy that views stages of the evolution of organic, chromatic functions as similar to stages in the morphology, that is, growth and development, of living, organic form and substance. Rather than the standard linear view, which tends to consider the development of historic styles to be determined by individual composers' contributions, I prefer the view that considers this development to be determined by significant nodal points in the overall growth process that lead to equally significant plateaus of maturation, where structural-organic coherence is brought to maximum realization through the collective efforts of generations of composers. The perfection of a particular tendency, form, or style of musical expression has often been slow, hard work, and its shapers are rarely conscious that they are part of a larger process. Because of its breadth and multiplicity of vision, this view permits us to see virtually everything significant in the last two centuries in a more integrated, comprehensive light.

From my point of view, the great value of this biological analogy is that it allows us to convert history into morphology without sacrificing what history has to offer: nodal points of morphological growth and development and plateaus of maturation can be placed along the timeline of historical movement. I am using "morphology" to mean the image of developing growth of organic, musical substance, and "history" to mean the visible line of movement of those stages of growth. By connecting the too-often one-dimensional movement of history firmly to the deeper strata of morphological growth over time, this analogy helps to guide us to more profound insights, and, I hope, to an awareness of the great energies and all-consuming intellectual-spiritual passions devoted to the pursuit of the realization of a particular line of musical endeavor. The long development of triadic harmony (from the fifteenth to the eighteenth century) leading finally to the remarkably flexible, fluid, and broad language of tonality is an excellent case in point. The achievement of the sonata form and its associated, if subsidiary, balancing forms (from the seventeenth to the nineteenth century) is another, not quite parallel, case in point. Together, both accomplishments—at the hands of countless composers—made possible the multimovement compositions conceived as large-scale organic wholes that provide performers with their repertoires.

The first great discernible plateau of fully realized growth and maturation is the modal system and its interlinking diatonic hexachords. The nodal points of its development include truly major achievements in Western music, among them the invention of musical notation, the codification of chant, systems of duple and triple meter, and the evolution of polyphony. This last led to the invention or discovery of imitation and counterpoint on the one hand, and to intervallic-harmonic incidence on the other. Some of these streams of discovery continued as fundamental aspects of musical composition in the next great plateau, the tonal system, feeding it the vital energies of the contrapuntal devices of canon and fugue, controlled now by powerful considerations of harmonic direction and function. If the modal system achieved full maturation in the fourteenth to fifteenth centuries, having been fed by streams of development beginning as early as the tenth century—and this is not taking into account any possible influence from the ancient Greeks on music theory or ancient Mesopotamian Valley cultures and Hebrews on chant—the tonal system (and its interlinking keys) attained full growth by the middle to the end of the eighteenth century, having gathered up a whole complex of evolutionary stages, now organized by the principle of a single key center as the generator of organic coherence.

One of the most significant stages must be the transformation from within the modal system of multiple church modes into the dual major-minor system of keys. The well-tempered tuning system, which permits smooth modulation from point to point on the circle of fifths, must also be counted among the important innovations that fed into the tonal system. Other important nodal points in the development of tonality are the evolution of monody, figured bass, and monophonic forms of melody and accompaniment.

All these developments occurred over time—some more rapidly, some more slowly. Of course, they can be described solely as history with all that historical telling entails—names, places, dates, persons, events, works, etc. But what this would miss is the sense that at levels below historical (and even sometimes below contemporaneous) awareness musicians are moved by deep passions to pursue certain directions, the ends of which they cannot necessarily see, but which bring to full maturation forms of musical expression that allow the human spirit to give voice to its highest and deepest spiritual and emotional experiences.

Were these great plateaus, which composers (mostly blindly) have helped to bring about, inevitable? Or were they purely accidental, the end product of collective groping in the dark? To believe that the great modal system and the great tonal system were inevitable is almost to suggest that *something* (how else does one refer to such an unknown?) was drawing these composers toward unforeseeably distant goals, guiding them in directions necessary to be able to say in music that which corresponds to the inner, ever-present sense and consciousness of world existence. Human beings—nature made conscious of itself—have always pursued with passion and energy the creation of musical structures eminently suited to their expressive needs. Rarely, if ever, have any of these forms of expression been accomplished in a brief span of time. And almost never has any form of expression been the creation of a single composer. The one exception is Arnold Schoenberg and atonality. But as we know now at the beginning of the twenty-first century, atonality, which sprang forth in a single generation (and in one time and place) and involved only three overlapping successive generations of composers to take it as far as it could be stretched, is no longer an independent organic entity of musical composition but is being absorbed into the wider stream of subsequent developments.

In order to tell the story of the emergence of symmetry from its diatonic sources in tonal music, and to trace its evolution to mature realization, parts 2 and 3 of the present work intend to make as clear as possible the plurality of organizing principles found in nineteenth-century music. Not only did harmonic functions expand dramatically, but chromaticism, long held in check by fundamental diatonic functions, broke loose and, by the middle of the century, emerged full-blown. At the same time temporal proportions expanded as a result of large-spanned, increasingly plastic and long-breathed melodic unfolding. Inevitably, the tonal enterprise became more and more tenuous, and the pristine clarity of eighteenth-century practice as manifested in Haydn and Mozart began to lose ground. The great time-spans of nineteenth-century music, starting with Beethoven's "Eroica," were made possible by the development of pluralistic principles of harmonic motion. Fundamental I–V–I relations, local and large-scale, were no longer adequate to the compositional situation, which itself was driven by the increasingly charged emotional and expressive intensity of composers. Structure, as Schoenberg has said, is not only the function of harmony, it is also the function of a larger time-sense; and, I would add, both interrelated functions absolutely depend upon the composer's way of shaping his emotional impulses and channeling his mental energies.

Once melodic phrases and shapes became more expansive, harmonic nodal points began to appear further and further apart structurally, and composers focused on internal details. The larger the projection or proportion in time of basic harmonic functions—for example, the twenty-measure-long dominant preparation for the recapitulation that Beethoven spins out in the first movement of the "Waldstein" Sonata, Op. 53—the greater the opportunity for imaginative unfolding of detail. The tension between this combination of basic structural simplicity and complexity of detail that grew as the nineteenth century wore on eventually overloaded the perceptual surface and weakened the sense of tonal direction.

A discussion of nineteenth-century music in general and chromaticism in particular must take into account pluralistic possibilities of description and explanation. Besides the I–V–I reductionism of Schenkerian analysis—which I am convinced is an oversimplification in the light of pluralistic factors offering multi- rather than unidimensional understanding—and besides the hierarchy of the essential step-functions of diatonicism, which traditionally determined key-centeredness, there is another principle of harmonic organization based on symmetrical orders subdividing both the octave and the circle of fifths that is independent of the traditional tonic-dominant hierarchy. This principle creates new harmonic relations that are enclosed in what I shall call circular harmonic sets (from time to time I shall also refer to them as symmetrical harmonic sets or closed harmonic sets), which are the focus of part 2.

Not only are there at least two great parallel orders of harmonic progressions to deal with—the traditional tonic-dominant asymmetrical diatonic order and the newly developed closed harmonic sets of a symmetrical order—but either one may, for purposes of expressing a local (or small-scale) progression or function, invoke the other, that is, bring its opposite into play. And within the symmetrical order, there are many arrays of sub-organization that expand the chromatic system toward greater richness, unexpected freedom of harmonic movement, and complexity of detail. We find that these two parallel but opposite orders, the one asymmetrical and therefore open-ended, the other symmetrical and therefore self-enclosed, may invoke the other in the following ways: large-scale I–V–I functions can (and often do) contain local, that is, small-scale, circular functions, and large-scale circular functions can (and usually do) contain local I–V–I functions. The interpenetration and irradiation of the two orders is what gives middle and late Beethoven, Schubert, Chopin, Brahms, and Wagner their particular aural flavor and color.

With the musical evidence before us as a grounding reality it would be totally illusory, if not self-deluding, to attempt to collapse these parallel polar opposites back into some arbitrary form of dualism or to reassert the old hegemony of the hierarchic asymmetrical I–V–I principle by trying to cram in chromatic symmetry in order to maintain a false unitary, monistic organicism. In fact, a system of harmonic relationships based on the polar opposites of an asymmetrical diatonic order and a symmetrical chromatic order is not necessarily less organic—in other words, coherent and unified—than a system based solely on monistic, diatonic organicism.

So long as the two parallel orders remain in consciously held balance, as they do, for example, in Brahms and Mahler—though obviously in different ways clear to both ear and eye—tonality remains a continuing, viable musical language. However, when the transformative powers of symmetrical chromaticism begin to take over, pushing out the asymmetries of traditional diatonic functions, the old tonal enterprise becomes endangered, and tonality—in order to preserve itself—begins the process of transformation into what we now call atonality.

Chapter Two

Diatonic Asymmetry, Enharmonic Spelling, and Multidirectionality

Before tracing the emergence of symmetry from its diatonic sources in tonal music, it is important to lay out the essentially asymmetrical nature of diatonicism by reviewing the relation to the diatonic steps of chromatic steps in the forms of two powerful functions—the leading-tone and the Neapolitan sixth. Equally important is an understanding of enharmonic spelling, a major consequence of which is multidirectionality. A survey of bi-, tri-, and tetradirectionality will close this preliminary discussion and set the stage for our first encounters in chapter 3 with circular harmonic sets.

When diatonic steps (I, II, III, IV, V, VI, VII) express root functions, chromatic steps may express leading-tone functions:

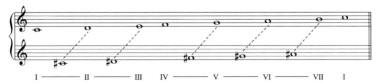

Example 2.1. Chromatic steps as leading-tones.

Because there is a half-step relation between III and IV and between VII and I, the leading-tone function may be invoked for III and VII in relation to IV and I as roots.

Chromatic steps may take on Neapolitan sixth function while diatonic steps retain root function:

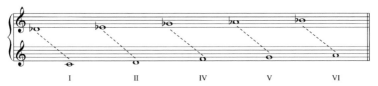

Example 2.2. Chromatic steps as Neapolitan tones.

Again, because there is a half-step relation between III and IV and between VII and I, IV and I may take on Neapolitan sixth functions in relation to III and VII as roots.

Thus each diatonic step may have two chromatic steps serving it: (a) *lower leading-tone,* in which case the chromatic step may be part of a dominant chord (secondary, tonicizing) or a diminished chord (tonicizing); and (b) *upper leading-tone,* in which case the chromatic step is the root of the Neapolitan sixth function.

When chromatic steps become root functions, diatonic steps become leading-tone functions, upper and lower:

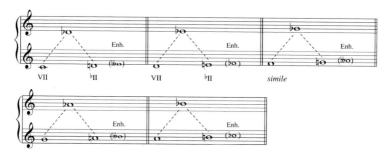

Example 2.3. Chromatic steps as roots.

Where a given key (major or minor) invokes chromatic steps, these functions are most often mixed.

In every case, there will be seven diatonic steps and five chromatic steps (or inflections). This basic pitch system is asymmetric, open, flexible. Since pitches may take on different functions in varying situations, they must be considered *relative* to function. Therefore, it is the functions, not the pitches, that are fixed and immutable. *Functions apply to pitches, not the other way around.*

Examples of the use of double leading-tones (both upper and lower) abound in the literature, functioning either as elements implying strong voice-leading in melodic passages—for example, in the F minor three-part Invention of J. S. Bach:

Example 2.4. J. S. Bach, 3-Part Invention No. 9.

And in the Beethoven String Quartet, Op. 59, no. 3, second movement, where the Neapolitan function is powerfully implied:

Example 2.5. Beethoven, String Quartet, Op. 59, no. 3, second movement.

And in the Beethoven "Moonlight" Sonata, Op. 27, no. 2, first movement, where the Neapolitan function is more fully expressed cadentially:

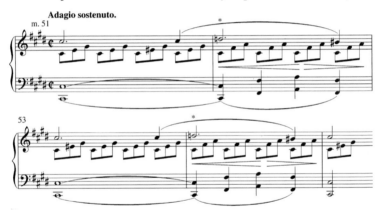

Example 2.6. Beethoven, "Moonlight" Sonata, Op. 27, no. 2, first movement.

Or as elements in large-scale melodic outlining of structural harmonic phrases, as in the openings of Beethoven's E minor String Quartet, Op. 59, no. 2, first movement, and his "Appassionata" Sonata for piano, Op. 57, first movement.

The appearance of upper and lower leading-tones in the same chord is especially potent in tonal harmony and signals the strongest possible voice-leading:

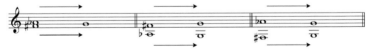

Example 2.7. Upper and lower leading-tones combined.

This combination of upper and lower leading-tones is the basis for the altered chords designated Italian, French, and German sixths. It is important to understand their derivations and implications since, in a fundamental way, they are chromatic intensifications of basic tendencies of diatonic step functions. These chords are used as frequently in the major mode as in the minor in nineteenth-century practice, confirming that the tonal system as it developed became a major-minor mixture evolving out of chromatic intensification of diatonic functions.

The following schematic brings together the three altered chords in successive harmonic motion to reinforce their differences yet their closeness:

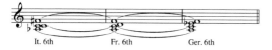

It. 6th   Fr. 6th   Ger. 6th

Example 2.8. The three altered chords.

When another inner voice is added to the Italian sixth to show smoother voice-leading in four parts, only one of the inner parts needs to move to establish each altered chord in turn, that is, the French sixth and the German sixth. All three chords thus have three pitches in common—A♭ and F♯ (the double leading-tones), and C—and one differing note.

There are other considerations that become apparent from a closer examination of the French sixth. These involve the internal structure of the French sixth, which points ahead to the twentieth century. First, the tritone relations inherent in the French sixth: A♭–D, C–F♯. Harmonic circularity is essentially governed by the symmetrical tritone, that is, a six-semitone division of the octave, while key (or tonal center) circularity is governed by the asymmetrical fifth of seven semitones. The consequences of this conclusion are very far-reaching indeed and must await further discussion in part 4.

Second, if we lay out the French sixth as a horizontal form and fill in the whole step spaces between A♭ and C with B♭ and between D and F♯ with E, we arrive at a whole-tone hexachord. Note that the filled-in pitches, B♭ and E, themselves form a tritone. Finally, it is possible to interpret the French sixth as a Neapolitan triad superimposed on the V of V:

Fr. 6th   N/V of V

Example 2.9. French augmented sixth as Neapolitan superimposed on the V of V.

We recognize example 2.9 immediately as the potential source of the "Petrouchka chord," a chord of superimposition of two major triads

a tritone apart. On further reflection we recognize that the "Coronation Scene" in *Boris Godunov* is one step removed from the "Petrouchka
chord": instead of sounding simultaneously as in the "Petrouchka
chord," the tritone-related chords of *Godunov* sound successively. We also
recognize that this six-note chord that Stravinsky "found" was already
anticipated in the finale of Schubert's "Great" C major Symphony where
measures 1057–72 and measures 1077–92 prefigure and foreshadow both
the *Godunov* succession and the "Petrouchka" simultaneity. Not surpris-
ingly—for Brahms was as bold a harmonist as the nineteenth century produced—there is in his Opus 117, no. 2, Intermezzo between measures 67
and 71 still another instance of tritone-related harmonic succession that
contains the elements of the "Petrouchka chord." This particular chord,
which Stravinsky "found," is a *compression* of basic harmonic functions
into a single harmonic unit.

There are two major implications of considerable significance arising out of our discussion of altered chords so far. First, the tonal system
is neither pure major nor pure minor but rather a major-minor mixture
developing out of chromatic alterations and combinations. Second, chords
begin to emerge that either imply, as in the case of the French sixth, or
state outright, superimpositions of two complete triads or significant elements of either or both to form new harmonic entities—or to imply their
eventual formation.

Enharmonic Spelling and Multidirectionality

Since functions apply to pitches and not the other way around, chromatic
harmony requires great care in spelling so that tonal direction is always
clear to the eye. The following makes it immediately apparent why ambiguity of direction readily applies to the ear. In fact, it is possible that
nineteenth-century composers understood this thoroughly and played on

ambiguity as a technical device. For example, 🎼 *sounded* does

not make clear whether we are hearing a German sixth in C major (or C

minor), or hearing 🎼 which, acting as a dominant, would resolve

to D♭ major or minor; or if we are hearing 🎼 which, as the same

dominant enharmonically respelled, would resolve to C♯ major or minor.

Or take the case of 🎼 which could easily resolve to

🎼 or 🎼 in which case the spelling of the French sixth

must be changed to read 🎼 .

Or take the case of [musical notation] which, depending on how it is spelled, can resolve in four directions.

Bidirectionality

Because enharmonic spelling allows for interpreting the resolution of tonicizing chords in more than one direction, new possibilities of tonal motion developed. As we saw above, the French sixth chord could be spelled two different ways: [musical notation] and [musical notation]. The clue to each of the different resolutions lies in the difference between the two sets of double leading-tones: double leading-tones $C^{\natural}$–$A^{\sharp}$ (in the first spelling) resolve to B, while double leading-tones $E^{\natural}$–$G^{\flat}$ (in the second spelling) resolve to F, a tritone away.

Inherent in French sixth bidirectionality lies the far-reaching significance of multidirectionality, the understanding of which is key to determining how symmetry developed in the heart of an essentially asymmetrical system. Without the possibility of multidirectionality, circular harmonic sets could not have developed as they did, nor would they have played such a large part in establishing the symmetrical principle of harmonic order and multiple-key relations paralleling the older principle of the dominant-tonic order and single key centers.

All altered chords are involved in multidirectionality. However, as we shall soon see, multidirectionality also includes in its vocabulary ordinary dominant sevenths and triads, as well as diminished chords.

Tridirectionality

Having established the conditions of bidirectionality, I want to take up tridirectionality, which can be produced via, first, the German sixth (ex. 2.10); second, the V^7 substitute for the German sixth (i.e., the German sixth respelled as a V^7, ex. 2.11); and, finally, the deceptive cadence (the traditional progression from V or V^7 to vi, whose normal function is to delay resolution to I, ex. 2.12). I shall illustrate each of these three approaches to tridirectionality in turn.

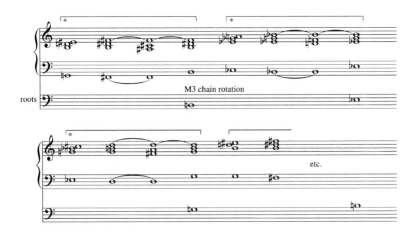

Example 2.10. Tridirectionality via German sixth.

Note that in the first approach to tridirectionality, the roots of the chords of resolution (B♮–E♭–G♯) outline an augmented triad. A chain rotation is set up resulting in a circular harmonic set that is governed by what I shall call a M3, that is, a major third step progression. Circularity (or symmetrical progression) does not abrogate the fundamental step-nature of diatonic tonal functions dependent on harmonic motion. On the contrary, it is primarily a reordering or repatterning of the same step progressions and therefore remains within the largely diatonically determined tonal system.

There is another way of unfolding tridirectionality via the German sixth, this time by employing the aural ambiguity of spelling each German sixth as a V^7 chord.

Example 2.11. Tridirectionality via German sixth, respelled.

Each sequence in the chain rotation is a contrapuntal filling-out of V^7 chords. The resultant harmonies of this filling-out produce their own secondary progression type. For example, the second and third beats of the opening measure of example 2.11 are themselves a *different* German sixth resolving contrapuntally to a *different* tonic $^6_4$. This interior harmonic detail repeats on other step degrees in the third and fifth measures of the example, making their own subset within the larger chain rotation. Note that the roots of the chain rotation in example 2.11 are the same as those in example 2.10.

The third method for producing M3 rotation is based on the traditional deceptive cadence. The M3-connected roots of the chain of deceptive cadences are *elisions* of these cadences:

Example 2.12. Tridirectionality via deceptive cadence.

We have here a perfect demonstration of the tonal system as a mixed major-minor mode. In B major the deceptive cadence is normally to vi, while in B minor it is normally to VI. When the V^7–vi (VI) progressions mix as they do in example 2.12 we hear the major mode substituting for the "normal" minor resolution. Consequently, no minor triads appear in this tridirectional chain based on the deceptive cadence. The chain rotation that binds the successive roots B♮–G♮–E♭ can go in any direction within the symmetrical chain starting from any point of the chain.

The device of mixing the minor-mode deceptive cadence with that of the major mode is relied on heavily by Mahler in the third and fourth movements of his Ninth Symphony:

Example 2.13. Mahler, Symphony No. 9, third movement.

Despite enharmonic respelling in measure 111 of example 2.13, Mahler is passing through deceptive cadence major-minor mode mixtures whose roots clearly outline an augmented triad: F♮–D♭–A♮.

It is important to point out that, although significantly different in resulting sound and the functions employed, all three demonstrations of tridirectionality confirm each other through their chain rotation through an augmented triad, that is, M3 motion.

Tetradirectionality

We move now to a discussion of tetradirectionality, that is, symmetrically rotating harmonic chains that produce four different roots. These four equidistant roots outline a diminished chord and will be referred to as a m3 progression, that is, a progression based on minor thirds. As we shall see, M3 and m3 progressions are crucial to the internal transformation of tonality brought about by the symmetrizing of chromaticism and are crucial as well in overcoming the traditional functions attributed to and inherent in the circle of fifths.

Our first approach to tetradirectionality is via the German sixth/V⁷ ambiguity. The ambiguity consists, we will recall, in the fact that a German sixth sounds to the ear like a dominant seventh chord; without the eye to guide it, the ear cannot distinguish the difference. The following illustrates the point of the ambiguity involved:

Example 2.14. Tetradirectionality via German sixth/V⁷ ambiguity.

The roots arrived at the end of each of brackets W, X, Y, and Z outline a diminished chord through equidistant minor thirds, that is, they form a m3 progression. Each root supports a V⁷ that never resolves to a so-called tonic but, following the pattern of the W progression, sequences through X and Y and Z at the end of which it returns to W. Quite literally this is an unbreakable chain—unless, for example, one uses any of the four $^6_4$ chords (in minor) to cadence to a "tonic" or some other method of breaking the chain and thus escape from the inexorable symmetry of the chain rotation. Also note that the opening chord of W, a German sixth, appears as the second chord after the repeat sign, but spelled as a V^4_2 whose root is E♮, one of the elements of the diminished chord underlying the entire circular harmonic set: C♯–B♭–G♮–E♮.

In another approach to tetradirectionality, the same circular harmonic set is produced in example 2.15 by resolving the four possible constituent forms (i.e., the four different spellings) of the diminished chord B♯–D♯–F♯–A♮. The resulting chords of resolution (C♯, E, G, B♭) are triads in root position, not dominant sevenths. Example 2.15 demonstrates that tetradirectionality is produced directly by the four possible chords of the same diminished chord respelled and functioning as changing vii°⁷–I resolutions.

Example 2.15. Tetradirectionality via four possible diminished seventh resolutions.

Observe that the order of nodal points (*) differs from the order of nodal points marked in example 2.14. This time, the chain rotation goes in contrary motion to the chain of example 2.14. The roots are bound to the same diminished chord and form a harmonic field that potentially closes itself off from asymmetric, open-ended diatonic functions—even though it makes use of exactly the same harmonic materials we find in the traditional tonal system. We are—with these symmetrical uses of older asymmetrical harmonic forms, for example, vii°⁷–I—on the threshold of an order of harmonic relationships that has other purposes relating to structural articulation than the earlier, more naive view of the circle of fifths, and that is the possible bridge to aspects of the new order of harmony in the music of the twentieth century. I do not intend to give the impression that the circle of fifths is abrogated, done away with, set aside; but rather, I am suggesting that there are new divisions of the circle of fifths that dispense with the assumption that all basic tonal motions can be reduced to V–I.

Next we turn to what I shall call an *infinite* chain rotation—infinite in the sense that there is no escape from its continuous Tetradirectional contrapuntal filling-out via the German sixth/V^7 link:

Example 2.16. Infinite chain, expanding.

The infinite expansion of the schema of example 2.16 is, of course, also contractible. To demonstrate this, example 2.17 contracts through a diminished chord other than the diminished chord that controls example 2.16:

Example 2.17. Infinite chain, contracting.

In "Marina's Air" from Mussorgsky's *Boris Godunov* we find an aborted chain rotation that touches on three of the four pitches of the diminished chord chain but does not complete the circularity.

Example 2.18. Mussorgsky, "Marina's Air" from *Boris Godunov*.

However, though the passage ends with the seventh measure, theoretically the circularity of the chain rotation could be completed by carrying the melodic and accompanimental design through the remainder of the expanding progression until the opening dominant seventh on G is reached again.

While I know of no compositional use of a complete infinite chain rotation as demonstrated in example 2.16 (and ex. 2.17), aspects or parts of such progressions are quite common in nineteenth-century music. This is illustrated in the following examples.

Example 2.19. Brahms, Symphony No. 2, first movement.

Example 2.20. Chopin, Mazurka, Op. 33, no. 4.

Example 2.21. Brahms, Scherzo, Op. 4, Trio II.

Part Two

Symmetry in Tonal Music

Chapter Three

Intimations of Circularity

Embryonic Circular Sets

In the following example we find one of Mozart's most astonishing musical and intellectual feats, as well as our first intimation of harmonic circularity to be more fully developed by his successors, Beethoven and Schubert in particular:

Example 3.1. Mozart, Symphony No. 41, fourth movement.

Example 3.1. Mozart, Symphony No. 41, fourth movement—*(concluded)*

We are so used to thinking of him as the fantastically spontaneous composer—almost like a force of nature—he obviously was that we tend to forget that, however intuitive and rapid his mental processes were, he was clearly fully conscious at all times of what he was doing. By the time he wrote his last symphony, he, of all his contemporaries, was pressing eighteenth-century harmonic thinking to the absolute limit—certainly one could say well into the nineteenth century and beyond.

In the music just prior to the passage in example 3.1, Mozart returned to his cantus firmus main theme (at m. 225), and after one statement of antecedent-consequent phrases he launches into an incredibly powerful extended reiteration of the cantus firmus (at m. 233) with two obbligato countersubjects, the top voice (woodwinds) essentially chromatic, the bass voice (low strings) supporting increasingly chromatic harmony with short, brusque partial scales so that by the time we get to measure 241, where example 3.1 begins, we are poised for the amazing climax of this extension of the cantus firmus through 21 measures.

The first aspect of what I find amazing is that there are three simultaneous levels of movement by fifths, all three by descending motion: (1) the five three-note chromatic rises played by the woodwinds in octaves, starting at measure 243, move through the flat side of the circle with beginning pitches at C, F, B♭, E♭, and A♭; (2) the upper of the two lines of alternating fifth motion (the bottom two staves in ex. 3.1) shows a series of descending fifths on the sharp side, starting at measure 244: E–A–D–G–C; (3) the lower of the two lines shows a series of descending fifths on the flat side: F–B♭–E♭–A♭–D♭. These three levels are the *result*, not the self-generating *cause*, of something else. It is this something else that constitutes the second aspect of what I find so remarkable about the passage. I am referring, of course, to the complexes of harmony that are the substance of the musical motion Mozart is generating around and through his extensions of the cantus firmus.

There are five two-measure units of cadential motion beginning at measure 243 that are the very essence of the harmony we need to understand. If we grasp the first of these two-measure units, we will have the key to what Mozart is doing. The first beat of measure 243 sounds an Italian sixth chord. This chord quickly enlarges to a German sixth with the first note (C) of the woodwinds' three-note chromatic rise on the second beat, with the result that the altered IV of A on the first beat is intensified on the second beat. The D$^\sharp$ is the altered root of both the Italian and German sixths and resolves to an E major chord (the first beat of measure 244) with C$^\sharp$ superimposed on it as a passing note to D$^\natural$. The D$^\natural$ immediately converts the chord of resolution to a dominant seventh on the second beat of measure 244. Thus the bass motion, F to E, against the woodwinds' contrary motion, C–C$^\sharp$–D, is the melodic model that governs the outer voices while altered chord resolutions to dominant sevenths govern the inside voices through measure 253. Now the third amazing aspect: the four-note head of the cantus firmus that Mozart pushes downward by whole steps—from E to D to C—where he is aiming all along—now becomes a canon at the fifth (!) to itself.

There remains only one last motion to understand, namely, that between the chords of resolution and the altered chords that follow directly. The approach to each altered chord is marked in the bass voice by a plunge to the tritone. This occurs four times before we reach the new motif at measure 253, so we know that Mozart *means* it. And in this abrupt drop to what for medieval theorists was the forbidden interval we have the fourth and final aspect, which I consider the most incredible, especially in the context of the eighteenth century.

Before I identify what this aspect is, it will strengthen my point to direct attention to the fact that at two particular junctures when the bass moves to the tritone, the cantus firmus line (played by the first violins) does the same, that is, moves melodically through a tritone. The first time this occurs is between measures 244 and 245, the second time between measures 248 and 249. Even though the tritone motions of the bass and the cantus firmus occur in contrary motion, presumably to offset an awkward parallelism (which would be too close a reminder of the taboo against parallel fifths), are such motions "lawful" in an age still bound by the tradition of Fux? The question of "lawfulness" intensifies as soon as one realizes that these motions in the soprano and bass parts are only details, albeit very important ones, of a harmonic progression between two successive dominant sevenths a tritone apart—even if the second dominant seventh is spelled like an altered chord:

Example 3.2. Dominant sevenths a tritone apart.

In effect, then, we have, in eighteenth-century terms, a completely "unlawful" progression that, as I have already mentioned, occurs three more times, in measures 246–47, 248–49, and 250–51.

Given our present retrospective vantage point from which we can view the whole harmonic panorama from Mozart to our own time, and our by now long experience of every conceivable vertical combination of pitches so that nothing shocks our ears, the tritone harmonies Mozart has produced nevertheless *do* shock us because we know the historical context in which they occur. They startle us even more when we recognize that this particular tritone progression of dominant seventh chords is *identical* to the harmonic foundation of the "Coronation Scene" of Mussorgsky's *Boris Godunov* and because we know, too, that this progression—presented successively—is the material out of which Stravinsky fashioned his "Petrouchka chord," a chord produced by the superimposition of the elements of two dominant sevenths a tritone apart.

Rather than try to exonerate Mozart from "unlawfulness," let us look a little deeper. It is perfectly true that measures 244–45 are irreconcilable with eighteenth-century harmony as they stand—that is, by themselves and out of context. However, if we return them to their context, we see immediately that between measure 244 and the chord of measure 246 is a perfectly plausible progression from E^7 to A^7, a properly functioning fraction of the circle. Lawfulness of motion is regained; but how to account for the intervening chord, the altered chord of measure 245? This turns out to be a garden-variety German sixth (on the second beat of the measure), which resolves quite naturally to A major or its dominant form. In fact, it is precisely the same German sixth cadence Mozart employed three times in a row in example 3.1. Still, the sting of E^7 to $B^{\flat 7}$ remains and needs further resolution in order for us to be completely satisfied.

Without anticipating the full-dress discussion of circular harmonic sets, which still lies ahead of us, it can be stated at this point that with this progression Mozart anticipated the emergence and future development of symmetrical harmony—of which his progression (repeated four times) is a forerunner. Establishing complete lawfulness for the earlier-than-expected appearance of this tritone-ruled progression rests entirely on the fact that this particular type of tritone progression by dominant sevenths belongs absolutely to a basic and significant circular harmonic set that was not yet to emerge fully until some fifty years after Mozart's death. What is truly amazing, then, about this passage, which exemplifies in so many astonishing ways movement along the circle of fifths, is that while its harmonic substance derived from standard devices of eighteenth-century harmonic thinking, its application profoundly anticipated what still lay ahead well into the middle of the nineteenth century. It suggests that as early as the end of the eighteenth century, tonality, although hemmed in by routine thinking to which composers like Haydn and Mozart were clearly exceptions, was beginning its gradual transformation toward symmetrical chromaticism and that the anomaly of symmetrical harmony in an asymmetrical diatonic system was already exerting its ultimately irresistible pressure, albeit in forms whose emergence remained unknowable even to those to whom, like Mozart, flashes of what Shelley called "futurity" occurred.

As circular harmonic sets establish new structural relations and corresponding functions, they form a system of relationships that parallels the V–I system, which is expressed as the largest unit of division of the circle of fifths. In symmetrical sets, each "tonic" is ideally provisional; that is, each provisional "tonic" in any given set, whether that set is m3 or M3, has the same value as any other "tonic" in the same set. Thus, the three tonics in a M3 set are equally important. The same holds true for the four tonics in a m3 set. This immediately distinguishes tonics of circular harmonic sets from *the tonic* (or home key) of a tonal composition, which sits at the head of a functional harmonic hegemony. And while this head tonic may temporarily relinquish control to other *secondary* tonics and *their* train of subordinate functions, including that of secondary dominants, the controlling tonic can always reclaim *in full* its primary power over the structure of a tonal composition.

The absolutism (within the limits suggested above) of the tonic in an asymmetrical diatonic tonal field, therefore, is of a totally different order from the "tonics" of symmetrical sets, which share power ideally and distribute it equally among themselves. No tonic of a M3 or m3 set can arrogate to itself more power than its symmetrical partners. In order to do so, symmetry would have to be broken and replaced by asymmetry, and should that happen, we are no longer talking about symmetrical chromaticism but about a chromaticism that relinquishes its independence and willingly submits to the asymmetrical control of diatonic functions. Suddenly, in this phenomenon of equivalently shared power among symmetrical tonics we see a possible, even probable, source of Schoenberg's equivalency principle for all twelve tones, which underlies atonality. This very principle is the heart of his description of twelve-tone composition as a method of "composition with twelve tones related only to one another."[1] Thus, intensification of chromaticism brings with it homogenization of harmonic values, even when the harmonies in question still derive from the tonal realm, although they operate symmetrically within the larger asymmetrical diatonic field. This becomes apparent even as we deal with embryonic sets—although with embryonic sets it will still be obvious that *the tonic* of a work has only temporarily withdrawn off-stage and is awaiting its cue to return front and center.

In Beethoven's String Quartet, Op. 130, we find a considerable length of durational space that he fills in ingenious ways. The first thing that strikes us as we read through the exposition of the first movement is how tightly Beethoven keeps the *Allegro* passages reined in harmonically, essentially working through I, V, or V^7 in B$^\flat$ until at measure 51 he rises from F by half-step motions straight up to D$^\flat$. From D$^\flat$ he drops in two brief diatonic figures through the scale of G$^\flat$ major to its tonic at measure 55 and begins his second thematic group in G$^\flat$ major, the major third submediant of B$^\flat$, which fills the remainder of the exposition, including the very brief closing section. In the first *Allegro*, respelled as F$^\sharp$ major (although he retains the G$^\flat$ major key signature), Beethoven restates the major third submediant at measure 96. In the *Adagio* that follows directly at measure 97, D major enters without preparation and remains through measure 113 (changing harmonically, through cancellation of C$^\sharp$ to C$^\natural$, from D major [I] to V^7 of G major, which is the next area of the still-ongoing development section).

Example 3.3 sketches the motions we have just discussed, through measure 105:

Example 3.3. Sketch of embryonic M3 circular set in Beethoven, Opus 130, first movement.

Example 3.3. Sketch of embryonic M3 circular set in Beethoven, Opus 130, first movement—*(concluded)*

It needs to be emphasized that Beethoven's use of the major mediant as the key of the second theme is no less a "true" musical event than if the second key were the conventional dominant. Beethoven's use of the major mediant *and* submediant is too much a part of his harmonic-structural vocabulary not to come to grips with. However we attempt to explain it, we cannot ignore the plain and audible-visible fact that the replacement of the dominant as the key of the second theme by the major mediant or submediant is a fundamental departure from earlier practice. And it is no less startling when Beethoven chooses to follow the first movement of his C minor Piano Concerto, Op. 37, with a slow movement in E major. In fact, in the opening piano solo we find a half-close cadence to G♯ major in measure 4, and at measure 9, at the beginning of the consequent phrase we are suddenly in G major! Perhaps this was utterly bewildering to the mind still chained to the doctrine of V–I, but it is precisely these kinds of major- and minor-third motions that we are discovering in embryonic symmetrical harmonic sets and, more particularly, in Beethoven's use of them.

I conjecture that the man who at nineteen had tested his organizing powers of harmony against the tight, relational symmetry of the circle of fifths (see his Opus 39) also must have taken special note of the mediant and submediant junctures between the ends of expositions and the beginnings of developments by Haydn and Mozart (see, for example, Haydn's

Symphony No. 97, first movement, mm. 106–12 and Symphony No. 98, first movement, mm. 130–40, and Mozart's "Jupiter" Symphony, first movement, mm. 120–25). It is possible that Beethoven recognized something of great structural import in those major and minor third juxtapositions. The play on the third so prominent in Opus 130 (and elsewhere) favors this probability—whether or not Beethoven consciously knew that he was working with harmonic symmetry *qua* symmetry, and that, in fact, he was among the very first to do so.

I turn now to one of those unrepeatable, completely unique gestures in early nineteenth-century music, a singular example of what I call "deathless moments," because they are, once experienced, unforgettable and burn themselves into one's soul. It is as though they speak not a universal, but an eternal, language. I am referring to that passage in the second movement, Andante un poco moto, of Schubert's G major String Quartet, Op. 161, starting at measure 43, which contains, albeit incomplete, one of the most incredible m3 rotating circular harmonic sets in the literature. I am devoting examples 3.4 through 3.8 to exploring the various levels contained in this powerfully expressive and intellectually complex passage.

Example 3.4. Schubert, String Quartet No. 15 in G Major, Op. 161, second movement.

One of the first things we can't help but notice is the utter obstinacy of the G–B♭ figure played three times by the first violin and the viola. We note especially the seemingly heedless, chaotic dissonances resulting in measures 54 and 56 between the reiterations of G–B♭ and the preceding chords and wonder what Schubert had in mind—beyond the powerful drama that is taking place musically. Why does he insist on G–B♭ though everything around the two-note figure is changing drastically? The clue lies in example 3.5.

The pitches G–B♭ have a certain harmonic ambiguity. That is to say, G–B♭ belong simultaneously to the G minor of measure 52 and to the diminished chords whose four possible spellings may be seen in example 3.7. There are essentially two harmonic interpretations of this passage. First, despite the fact that G–B♭ belong to the diminished chords implied in the tremolandi of measures 53, 55, and 57 and help to complete those chords, what we hear is not G–B♭ absorbed into the implied diminished chords but G–B♭ as the essential minor third of G minor sounding through regardless of the i_4^6–V resolutions of measures 54 and 56 in completely distant and disagreeing harmonic regions. The second interpretation is that because G–B♭ are absorbed into the successive pitches that follow directly on each iteration, they lose their identity as G minor and, despite the i_4^6–V resolutions that follow, stubbornly maintain their character as elements of the diminished chords to which they belong. Stated another way, the first interpretation claims the continued implied sounding of G minor, and the second interpretation claims the continued implied sounding of the diminished chord G–B♭–C♯–E. These two interpretations can be shown still another way as imagined continuous layers of sound:

Interpretation 1
   Layer 1: G–B♭ as G minor
   Layer 2: Diminished chord G–B♭–C♯–E
   Layer 3: i_4^6–V resolutions: C♯ minor, B♭ minor, G minor, and the unstated but completing member of the m3 set, E minor—the roots of their respective triads collectively making up the same diminished chord as layer 2

Interpretation 2
   Layers 1/2: G–B♭ absorbed into diminished chord G–B♭–C♯–E
   Layer 3: same as interpretation 1

My own preference is for interpretation 1, which provides maximum possibilities for harmonic intensity and therefore emotional intensity. The problem with interpretation 2 is that G minor disappears except as the third i_4^6–V resolution, and G–B♭ are completely absorbed into the diminished chords, removing the clanging, stinging quality of G minor against the second and third layers. In short, interpretation 2 possesses too much internal agreement and therefore loses its dramatic and emotional power.

In each example from 3.5 through 3.7 I have completed the full implications of a m3 circular harmonic set but have bracketed off the last one, which Schubert does not use. The four possible directions of resolution of a diminished chord are shown for completion's sake in order to reinforce two points: first, that the resolutions of example 3.6, if completed to the respective i in each case, would produce roots that, as already noted above, would make up the diminished chord Schubert does use: C#–B♭–G–E; and second, that the bass of each chord, stated or implied, that is, i_4^6 or V or i, is itself part of a rotating m3 set. The set of the bass notes of the respective i_4^6 chords is G#–F–D–B; of the respective V chords is the same as i_4^6; and of the respective i chords (implied) is C#–B♭–G–E. We can see (hear?) at a glance why G–B♭ sounding insistently against chords whose bass notes and roots are the same in each of the rotating i_4^6–V progressions and composing a different diminished chord from the one Schubert actually uses strengthen interpretation 1: that is, had Schubert completed each resolution i_4^6–V to its respective i, he would have reinforced the diminished chord that contains G–B♭, thus weakening the clash he sought. This discussion can be checked further against the other passages where the same relationships occur but on other pitches: F# minor, beginning at measure 72 and ending at measure 80, and D minor, beginning at measure 131. Finally, I want to take special note of example 3.8, which introduces to our discussion of symmetry in chromaticism the eight-note or octatonic scale. Suffice it to say, for now, that the pattern of alternating tones and semitones is the scale of the generic diminished chord. In Schubert's passage we see (and hear) the unique color of the octatonic scale, which has a long history through compositional practice in the nineteenth and twentieth centuries. It is fundamentally implied by rotation through minor third melodic or harmonic motion. We shall return to this later.

Example 3.5. Model of m3 circular motion completed.

Example 3.6. Model of resolutions of m3 circular motion.

vii°⁷/V   i $\frac{6}{4}$ V

Example 3.7. Tetradirectionality of diminished chord.

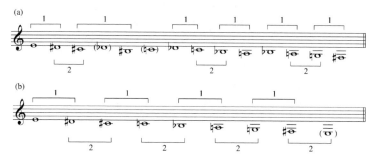

Example 3.8. Extracting the octatonic scale.

Chapter Four

More Evolved Circular Sets

Chopin's music provides another rich source of M3 and m3 sets, some of which reach a degree of perfected realization that is the sign of full maturity and are, therefore, the next logical step after Schubert in tracing the evolution of symmetrical chromaticism in tonal music.

Things get more complex with Chopin. Whereas Beethoven and Schubert succeed in overcoming the dominance of the dominant but remain—despite their advances into chromaticism—essentially diatonic composers (albeit casting their diatonicism in larger, more open structural frames), Chopin's temperament and sensibilities lead him deep into chromaticism, but not necessarily away from the diatonic. Chopin is the first of several major composers of the nineteenth century to work clearly and consciously on the diatonic and chromatic levels simultaneously. The forms Chopin worked with—essentially dance and song forms—made thematic distinction crucial to grasping the formal succession, variational development, and recapitulation of his ideas. Given this necessity, diatonicism and chromaticism as opposites were perfect foils for one another, and Chopin treated them as such—as did Brahms and, to a certain extent, Mahler. In the study of Chopin, the search for an expressive balance between diatonicism and chromaticism must be kept in mind at all times.

Examples 4.1 and 4.2, both from Chopin's Ballade in F Major, Op. 38, could not be more different from each other.

Example 4.1. Chopin, Ballade in F Major, Op. 38, mm. 62–68.

Example 4.2. Chopin, Ballade in F Major, Op. 38, mm. 107–10.

Example 4.1 is a sequential pattern by fifth motions that progresses from A^7 to its tritone E^{b7} through C^7. Example 4.2 is a quick chromatic run through the diminished chord E–G–B^b–C$^\sharp$. (A similar parallel passage on a different diminished chord, E^b–F$^\sharp$–A–C, occurs later in the same developmental context beginning in the second half of measure 132.) On closer inspection, we realize that each passage is a different way of expressing the same m3 circular harmonic set, A–C–E^b–F$^\sharp$, and quickly note that in example 4.1, F$^\sharp$, the fourth member of the m3 set, is missing, making for an incomplete set. (In example 4.2, all members of the set are present.)

Because example 4.2 is actually more complex than appears on the immediate surface, I have written out in example 4.3 two different harmonic models of m3 sets that are embedded in the passage from measure 107 through the first four beats of measure 110. There are three harmonic levels at work in this passage: the first, and the only one not needing an explanation, is the reiteration on the first and fourth beats of each measure (beginning with the half-measure of 107) of the diminished chord that underlies the passage, E–G–B^b(A$^\sharp$)–C$^\sharp$; the second, the m3 series of chords of example 4.3a (written in whole notes); and the third, the different m3 series of chords of example 4.3b (also in whole notes).

Example 4.3. Models of m3 sets embedded in mm. 107–10.

A number of small but important anomalies need to be mentioned here in connection with spellings of some notes and with one particular note not stated in example 4.3a. First, the second chord of example 4.3a, which has A$\sharp$ in the bass, must be reinterpreted: the A$\sharp$ should be respelled as B$\flat$ to place the chord in the context of this particular m3 symmetrical set. Obviously, A$\sharp$ is Chopin's own spelling and belongs to the underlying diminished chord. Chopin himself switches to the B$\flat$ spelling on the next beat (the fourth) of measure 108 (see ex. 4.2). My reason, however, for respelling A$\sharp$ as B$\flat$ is to make clear its V$_2^4$ inversion, which is the same inversion as the last chord of measure 109. It is in this last chord that C$\sharp$ is not stated, perhaps because Chopin felt that the C$\sharp$ octave in the left hand on the previous beat of the measure (the fourth) carried over. However, for clarity's sake I have included C$\sharp$ in brackets in the A$_2^4$ chord. Another anomaly in spelling occurs on the third beat of measure 109, where B$\flat$ should be respelled as A$\sharp$ to make it conform to the F$\sharp$ chord in the set.

The pattern of the chords in example 4.3a—all major—would then be interpreted as follows: A$_4^6$–C$_2^4\sharp$–E$\flat{}_4^{b6}$–F$_4^{\sharp6}\sharp$–A$_2^4$. In other words, a complete rotation through the m3 set, arriving back at its starting point, A.

Example 4.3b shows another set of chords—all minor with the exception of the fourth chord in the series—rotating through a m3 set different from the one in example 4.3a, and linking the last chord to the first, C$\sharp$ minor. This different symmetrical set, C$\sharp$–E–G–B$\flat$, turns out to be a form of Chopin's underlying diminished chord that binds these m3 sets together. The pattern of the chords of example 4.3b then is: C$\sharp$ minor^6–E minor $_4^6$–G minor–B$\flat$ major^6–C$\sharp$ minor. I believe the anomaly of the fourth chord in the series, B$\flat$ major^6, with D$\natural$ in the left hand, not D$\flat$, can be explained by Chopin's decision not to anticipate the C$\sharp$ of the F$\sharp$ major chord that follows, even though it breaks the consistency of the minor mode of the series. (Using D$\natural$ in the E–D–C$\sharp$ figure of measure 109 also preserves the left-hand pattern established by the C$\sharp$–B–A$\sharp$ figure of measure 108.)

The only way to savor the difference between the two models in example 4.3 is to play them through slowly a number of times. They should then be put in context again by playing the passage as Chopin wrote it (ex. 4.2). Taken up to speed—*stretto più mosso*—one realizes the kaleidoscopic nature of such an assemblage of consecutive harmonies whose sole function is to flesh out the diminished chord laid out as a chromatic scale in the right hand supported by the skeleton of the pitches of the diminished chord in the left hand. The brilliantly colored harmonic blurring that results, the whole played *f* crescendoing to *ff* as Chopin wrote it, is already at the edge of chromatic overload, just short of becoming psychologically—if not aurally—nontonal. Chopin's taste and judgment ensure that such passages are brief, transitional—and therefore even more effective than if they were allowed to go on too long—and stand between more stable, harmonically functional areas. Harmonic function is important, for, even though we can identify two different m3 symmetrical sets (the two sets presented in the "roots" staves of exx. 4.3a and 4.3b) as harmonic chains, they are completely subsumed under the larger function of the diminished chord, through which they rotate. Therefore, in spite of the logic of their rotation, which has been demonstrated, while they are in no sense incidental, neither are they in any real sense harmonically functional. Such a passage as example 4.2 stands then as an exception to the rule, for circular harmonic sets normally have function with respect to tonal direction and structural, local, or large-scale design, as we shall further discuss later.

In direct contrast to the knotty passage from the Ballade in F Major, the next example from Chopin's Mazurka in C♯ Minor, Op. 50, no. 3 is a perfectly and fully realized m3 symmetrical set, a clear-cut, beautifully fashioned instance of rotation.

Example 4.4. Chopin, Mazurka in C♯ Minor, Op. 50, no. 3.

Asterisks mark off the harmonic vertebrae of this set based on the diminished chord B–D–F–G♯. Rotation through the set occurs two and a half times, from the cadence in B major at measure 159 to the first beat (D major) of measure 171. Chopin breaks the third rotation to push to C♯ minor $^6_4$ (m. 173), from which he moves to the conclusion of the piece. The symmetrical set, then, takes place after all the thematic content has been expressed and serves the function of an animated, harmonically intensified coda beginning in C♯ minor (m. 157) moving urgently and chromatically through rapid kaleidoscopic harmonic changes to C♯ minor $^6_4$ (m. 173), from which Chopin makes his descent to the final tonic cadence at measure 192. The phrase lengths within the rotations of the set are unequal: two measures to the first cadence in B major; two measures to the cadence in D major; one measure each from D major to F major to G♯ major to B major to D major; again two measures from D major to F major, two from F major to G♯ major; and one measure each from G♯ major to B major to D major.

Obviously, it is in the one-measure units where harmonic change speeds up perceptibly, and in the two-measure units where it seems to slacken and stretch momentarily. The patterns of harmonic progression from cadential node to cadential node differ sufficiently between the one- and two-measure units so that the passage from measure 157 through measure 171 is kept from merely sounding like contrary-motion chromatic passing notes between the outer voices.

Example 4.4 is our first instance of multiple rotation; that is, rotation through the circular harmonic set occurs more than once in direct succession, in this case two and a half times. As with all historical movements of great significance, it is not always possible to say exactly when something begins; one cannot always assign a precise time or place. This applies to the emergence of multiple rotation. Barely begun in the music of Schubert, it becomes clearly evident in the work of Chopin and later composers. Its significance for the development of musical composition is two-fold. First, out of the practice of multiple rotation developed the *harmonic field*; that is, tonal locus, *place* (terms discussed more fully in chapter 6). A more static concept of harmony replaced harmonic directionality, that is, motion toward a near or distant goal viewed as structural function. Second, it is impossible to escape the connection between rotation in the symmetrical tonal realm and rotation in the symmetrical atonal realm. To see multiple rotation in tonal music almost a century before we see it as one of the essential characteristics of twelve-tone music is to become aware of an inevitable development, namely, the eventual incorporation of symmetrical properties and functions into a method of composition that rests solely on relations between the notes themselves. As symmetry and rotation are virtually synonymous, symmetry in tonal music had to develop, as it did with Chopin, multiple rotation within the frame of the diatonic realm. The idea of passing from one harmonic vertebra of a symmetrical set to another in succession more than once is, *in principle*, exactly the same as passing from one to another of the twelve tones in successive patterns of motion. Of course, the differences are very great and are not to be set aside. Besides the obvious differences that I need not enumerate here, there is one difference that can only be expressed as an intuitive insight: namely, that the relative speed of rotation in symmetrical tonal music (such as ex. 4.4) as compared with, say, the relative speed with which the twelve tones are rotated in twelve-tone music, is much slower, more stately, even—as though one were observing moons orbiting a very large planet like Jupiter or Saturn. The reason, while obvious enough, nevertheless needs to be stated: tonal symmetrical rotation must still deal with the more cumbersome—but only from the point of view of the comparison—"machinery" of the old diatonic world, which inevitably causes it to slow down so that cadences from harmonic node to harmonic node can be clearly established. In twelve-tone music there is no preexisting harmony to deal with—other than that which the particular arrangement of those tones produces according to conscious decisions taken by the composer—so that, whether disposed vertically or horizontally or both, the round of twelve pitches can rotate with relatively great speed.

The relatively slow speed at which nodal points may be deployed in tonal music can be readily seen in example 4.5, a passage from Brahms's Second Symphony that is the last large structural phrase—leading to the recapitulation of the fourth movement—of a development section that itself is built on a large-scale M3 symmetrical plan, the beginning and end points of which are D major, the key of the movement:

m. 155	206	214	221	244
D (I) –	F♯ (III) –	B♭ (♭VI) –	F♯ (III) –	D (I)

The F♯ major passages use essentially the same motivic, harmonic materials, but the materials are varied according to their relative positions in the developmental plan. The function of the second of the two passages in F♯ major is to bring about a quiet return to the chief ideas of the movement, which is accomplished through Brahms's typically inverted structural psychology; that is, instead of resorting to the more conventional, strenuous *f* recapitulation, he drops the music to a whisper at measure 234, that is, ***pp***, the overall dynamic of example 4.5 being *p* from measure 221 on.

Example 4.5. Brahms, Symphony No. 2, fourth movement.

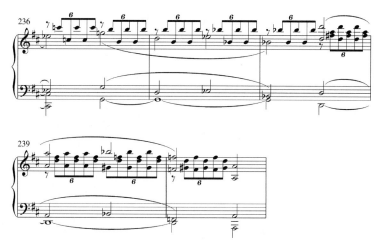

Example 4.5. Brahms, Symphony No. 2, fourth movement—*(concluded)*

Two basic devices of harmonic motion are used to move from F♯ major (m. 221) to D major (I) at the recapitulation (m. 244), the one a seemingly incomplete m3 symmetrical set, the other a very small portion of the circle of fifths, which, starting at C, comes to rest on A—but treated as though it were V of D minor, not D major. The m3 symmetrical set is *seemingly* incomplete because only three of its harmonic vertebrae are contiguous with each other: F♯ (both major and minor), A (also major and minor, and totally lacking any sense of being a dominant or even a pre-echo of the dominant to come), and C (major). E♭ is *not* contiguous with the other three members of the set, although it does appear in passing in the first inversion with G in the bass (mm. 237–38) as an aspect of the circle of fifths run that leads to the dominant. The question we will have to consider is: does the E♭, even in its first inversion, count as the fourth member of the symmetrical set while it does double duty as an aspect of the circle of fifths motion?

It is necessary to search out the small-scale harmonic motions that are the musical substance of the m3 symmetrical set—leaving aside for the present the question of its completeness or incompleteness—as well as the harmonies that reference the melodic material of the B♭ minor passage of the grand M3 set of the whole development as they occur at each node of the circle of fifths.

What we discover is that Brahms has locked into each pair of the four measures that express F♯ major, under the guise of neighbor notes and appoggiatura chords, a complete M3 set that is a mirror of the grand macroset that structures the whole development section: F♯ major–D minor mixed with major–B♭ major. As example 4.6 shows, the process is repeated in A major with other resulting harmonies. Because spellings are determined by the exigencies of melodic voice-leading, the harmonies that emerge are difficult to read vertically, so I have given their equivalencies in more conventional (though not better from the point of view of voice-leading) spelling.

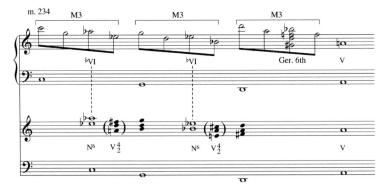

Example 4.6. M3 micro-mirror of macro-set of development section.

The micro-set in measures 227–30, A major–F major/minor–D♭ major, parallels the micro-set in measures 221–24, F♯ major–D major/minor–B♭ major, both sets composing the interior harmonic details of the large-scale m3 symmetrical set that breaks off at C major. What example 4.6 shows are the smaller, repetitive M3 symmetries embraced within the larger m3 symmetry. To say the least, this is a most unusual interweaving of both symmetrical sets—and, as far as I know, utterly unique in the literature.

We have yet to deal with the interior harmonic details of the circle of fifths motion from C major (m. 234) to D major (I), the beginning of the recapitulation. As example 4.7 shows, the principal harmonic result of the melodic motion over each ascending fifth is (again) a M3 symmetrical motion—except this time no set is completed. Be that as it may, Brahms maintains the continuity and consistency of treatment of the micro-mirror of the grander macro-set that structures the development.

Example 4.7. Continuation of M3 micro-mirror.

In order to understand better the connections that occur between the incomplete M3 micro-sets on C and G, first, I have interpreted the A♭ first inversion as a Neapolitan sixth of G, the resolving V$_2^4$ obviously imagined but unsounded, therefore elided, but nevertheless understood as the harmonic link in the fifth motion from C to G; second, I have interpreted the E♭ first inversion in parallel fashion to arrive at the harmonic link between G and D. Brahms himself "interprets" the fifth motion between D and A so that we need not attempt any interpretation of our own; it is spelled out very clearly.

We are left now only with one matter still unresolved, and that is the question I raised earlier: whether the brief appearance of E♭ major as an aspect in passing of the circle of fifths motion qualifies it as the fourth, therefore completing, member of the m3 set that starts with F♯ major. Part of our consideration of this question must now include the fact that E♭ is a member of a local, but incomplete, M3 set (mm. 237–38). While one condition, the fact of its belonging to a M3 set, complete or incomplete, does not preclude the other possible condition, that of its being the completing member of a m3 set, the fact remains that the appearance of E♭ is in no way contiguous with F♯–A–C, nor does it provide the same kind of harmonic "container" as do F♯ and A, let alone the much different kind provided by C. Everything militates against accepting E♭ as the completing member of the m3 set: its lack of contiguity; its appearance as a local detail in an incomplete M3 set; *as well as* that detail of being a passing aspect of a circle of fifths motion. Notwithstanding, this entire passage (ex. 4.5) remains exemplary for its role in the larger developmental context, particularly for the way in which its large-scale motions—the m3 symmetrical motion and the circle of fifths motion—enfold micro-M3 sets. In short, Brahms's personal brand of chromaticism is very much wrapped up with the principles of tonal symmetry, the very sound of his music often taking its particular colors from his handling of M3 and m3 circular harmonic sets.

Much the same thing can be said of Wagner as I have just said of Brahms—the great difference between them, however, being their totally distinct personalities, musically and psychologically, and, therefore, artistically. As we shall soon see, Wagner is as involved in the uses of symmetrical sets as Brahms; but while what each does with symmetry is essentially the same because of the inherent logic of circular harmonic sets, Wagner's uses of symmetry take on their own particular color and aural flavor. These differences can be heard because tonal symmetries are audible—and with practice, identifiable as to whether they are governed by m3 or M3 principles of organization. Tonal symmetry, whether in the hands of a Brahms or a Wagner, remains true to the best traditions of tonality of whatever period: it is music for the ear, it can be heard.

The examples I have drawn from Wagner to illustrate his use of symmetrical sets come from *Parsifal*, his last opera. Example 4.8 starts with measure 44 of the prelude and shows a fairly straightforward sequential use of an incomplete m3 set.

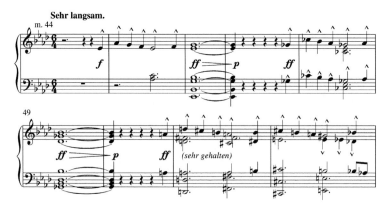

Example 4.8. Wagner, Prelude to *Parsifal*, mm. 44–52.

This first announcement of the Good Friday music in the opera is a particularly mechanical progression through a m3 sequence. Even under purely diatonic conditions, sequential motion runs the risk of taking on a dead rigidity, but motion by m3 where each phrase completes itself before moving on to the next harmonic level, matching phrase to harmonic level (particularly, as in this case, when enunciated in a declamatory fashion), particularly bogs down.

Its simplistic nature notwithstanding, two new conditions are worth pointing out: first, the subsidiary M3 motion that links $E^\flat$ (V) and $C^\flat$ (I), a motion that repeats itself throughout the rotation; and second, the new diminished chord based on the successive dominant resolutions, $E^\flat$–$G^\flat$–$A^\natural$. What saves the declamatory Good Friday music passage from mere mechanical repetitiveness is the "law of three," that is, the intuitive sense that has apparently operated in musicians for centuries that the third time for any sequence was the point to move out into something that brought new interest. Wagner solves this problem by using the D major phrase at measure 51 to begin a *new* sequence, which on *its* third repetition augments its durational values to finally cadence in a solemn $E^\flat$ minor (not shown).

We turn now to the chief melodic material of the prelude, which is perhaps one of Wagner's most beautifully formed melodic ideas. After several statements of this principal idea and approximately 35 measures of the Good Friday music, the principal idea with which the prelude opens comes again, this time intensified through m3 symmetrical set treatment, in fact, the same $A^\flat$–$C^\flat$–$D^\natural$–$F^\natural$ set underlying example 4.8.

Example 4.9. Wagner, Prelude to *Parsifal*, mm. 80–93.

Once again the "law of three" seems to operate: on the third of the three sequential rises—speaking *melodically* only—through A♭–C♭–D♮, instead of maintaining the symmetry of major keys, Wagner breaks away from D major into D minor, and, at the same time, extends the phrase in directions not previously touched on. We begin to ask ourselves how we are going to deal with the question of the "missing" fourth member of the set—whether F major or F minor. The question arises, first, because the "law of three" forecloses the possibility of extending a sequence of phrases such as this beyond its third variant form; and second, because while the implied harmony of the initial melodic line is clearly A♭ major—composed of an outlined triad followed by the diatonic steps leading to the upper A♭—Wagner harmonizes it with the lowest register minor third, F–A♭ (mm. 80–81). It is this interval that suggests either that "F" as F minor is present in the set, albeit in a new way, or that the A♭ major of the melodic phrase forms a two-tiered combination with F minor—not a completely hopeless conjecture since A♭ major and F minor are, in the old tonal world, *relative* to each other. The logic of the m3 symmetrical set being what it is, if we decide that the initial phrase is in F minor, despite the A♭ major character of the melody, then A♭ major as the first member of the set is now missing, and we have only F minor, C♭ major, and D minor. However, if we decide that the two-tiered combination of A♭ major/F minor is real, then we are in a position to satisfy our need for at least the *symbolic* presence of all the members of the m3 set. However one decides this issue, ultimately we have to keep in mind that whenever a m3 symmetrical set is invoked in the sequential repetition of a melodic phrase or phrases, the "law of three" obtains, and more often than not the set will be missing its fourth member. Our next example from *Parsifal* is taken from the prelude to Act II.

Example 4.10. Wagner, Prelude to *Parsifal*, Act II.

The pungent color of this passage is due entirely, I believe, to casting this M3 set with minor triads. Whether the triad members of a M3 circular harmonic set are in the major or minor mode, the collection they form has six pitches. Harmonic *color* in the sense we are discussing here is a very real option among symmetrical possibilities and one of which all nineteenth- and early twentieth-century composers who made use of symmetry took full advantage. In fact, the mixture of major and minor modes in symmetrical harmony produces still another variety of harmonic color, as illustrated by this passage from Act II of *Parsifal*:

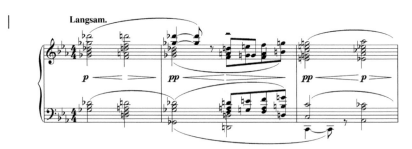

Example 4.11. Wagner, *Parsifal* (Parsifal: "Es starrt der Blick dumpf auf das Heilgefäß").

This is a curious instance of a strictly local M3 motion between G♭ major and D minor, combined with a similar motion between C major and A♭ minor, a harmonic unit that could be said to belong to elements of another M3 set. The expressive, emotional effectiveness of symmetrically organized harmonic color is again an audible perception. That is, one need not necessarily know the logic behind the aesthetic effect; one simply responds directly in the same way one takes in colors through the eye without knowing anything about theories of color perception.

Brahms and Wagner may not have consciously known—that is, been able to describe, to talk about in logical terms—the theory of the symmetries they were working with, but each possessed those mental and spiritual powers that gave him intuitive knowledge of, and therefore control over, the forces he was dealing with. While these forces can be made endlessly subject to analytic thinking, the real danger lies in losing sight of the qualitative side of the music, which is more important. While it may be true that logic inheres in the material and artistic forms of reality, these very forms (whether of Nature or of Man) are best apprehended *qualitatively*. This qualitative apprehension precedes quantitative comprehension understood as forms of analysis or science, and the relation between qualitative perception and quantitative, logical comprehension is that of primary to secondary levels of experience. Otherwise, why would we want to understand the reason for anything we experience?

Chapter Five

Fully Evolved Circular Sets

In this chapter we will analyze a group of pieces that exhibit artistic uses of the fully evolved circular harmonic sets. Each reveals a highly developed awareness of the *functional* possibilities inherent in the symmetry of these sets and therefore full consciousness—in an imaginative sense—on the part of the composers involved.

Chopin's G major Nocturne, Op. 37, no. 2 is remarkable not only for its imaginatively conceived uses of both the M3 and m3 sets but also for their crystal clear delineation of thematic contrast and structural layout. I am convinced that the division of this 139-measure piece into contrasting A and B thematic groups is the result of Chopin's conscious decision to compose a piece in which the symmetrical sets—one wonders what he called them, if anything, and how he thought of them—have specific thematic identification: m3 as a significant, *determining* harmonic factor of thematic group A, and M3 as the sole harmonic determinant of group B. In the rondo-like alternations of A and B groups, Chopin moves through so many keys at such a rapid rate of change that, without any understanding of how circular harmonic sets and their symmetrical principles work, it is virtually impossible to grasp what is happening tonally.

The texture and pianistic style of A, the first thematic group, is established immediately.[1]

Example 5.1. Chopin, Nocturne in G Major, Op. 37, no. 2, mm. 1–5.

Having stated the six-measure essence of his first idea, Chopin begins at measure 7 to make use of the m3 symmetrical set, giving only the first three members: G major (m. 7)–B♭ major (m. 8)–D♭ major (m. 9).

Example 5.2. Chopin, Nocturne in G Major, Op. 37, no. 2, mm. 7–10.

Each occurrence of A will contain both asymmetrical diatonic motions, as exemplified in the first six measures, and symmetrical rotation, as in measures 7–9. Group A begins to dissolve in mixed chromatic-diatonic motions with the upbeat to measure 26 and comes to temporary harmonic rest on E minor (m. 28), a new, berceuse-like melodic motion of the simplest possible nature beginning over it and continuing across the harmonic motion to C major (m. 30). The arrival at C presages the beginning of the M3 set, although thematic group B itself can be said to have begun two measures earlier. As example 5.3 shows, the C major melody turns very quickly to its first repetition in E major, which Chopin establishes by the simplest of means: moving to the vi of C major followed by its V (or III in C major).

Example 5.3. Chopin, Nocturne in G Major, Op. 37, no. 2, mm. 28–39.

C–E are paired major keys, forming two members of an incomplete M3 set. The technique by which Chopin introduces the third member of this set is ingenuity itself. We shall see how it is done very shortly.

To grasp fully how Chopin works the sets to maximum advantage, we need to see the structural layout of the work. Our next step, therefore, is to show this via a schematic:

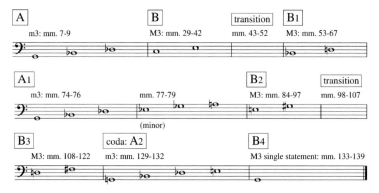

Example 5.4. Schematic of structural layout of sets.

Our first priority is to find out how Chopin uses the m3 set. The reason for its initial incompleteness, that is, for his not going on to E major, may or may not have anything to do with the "law of three." A better reason is that Chopin is saving E major for his first use of the M3 set in thematic group B. A still better reason is that, at the very outset of the piece, Chopin establishes an important tritone relationship between G major and D♭ major that necessarily rules out E major at this particular juncture. The importance of the tritone relationship lies, I believe, in Chopin's own awareness of the nature of the m3 set and his desire to emphasize its characteristic color, which is the outlining of the diminished chord and the fact that it contains two tritones, G/D♭–B♭/E. The tritone G/D♭ becomes tantamount to a fingerprint of thematic group A, its harmonic signature so to speak. This harmonic fingerprint or signature is developed in the parallelism between the progression in G major in the first phrase of the piece, measures 3–7, and the identical progression in D♭ major, measures 9–13.

The next appearances of m3 sets, measures 74–76 and 77–79, are somewhat more complicated. After a six-measure pedal point on D starting at measure 68, over which he repeats (with no change in figuration in the right hand) the harmonic progression of the opening phrase of the piece, Chopin reiterates the incomplete m3 set G–B♭–D♭, and, once he reaches the E♭ minor (ii of D♭), he begins what could be interpreted as another incomplete m3 set, this time E♭ minor–G♭ major–A major. A far simpler explanation, of course, would be that the passage from measures 76 to 78 is merely an elaboration of D♭ (I), which becomes V to G♭ major. This explanation, however, would erase the potency of E♭ minor as the beginning of the parallel incomplete m3 set in this passage, leaving only an unanchored minor third motion between G♭ major and A major. Given these several choices, I would prefer the interpretation that grants m3 status to

$E^\flat$ minor–$G^\flat$ major–A major principally because it preserves the device of motion by fifths that Chopin establishes in the m3 set of measures 7 to 9 (see ex. 5.5) and repeats in measures 74 to 76 and that remains a characteristic of thematic group A throughout the piece.

Example 5.5. Motion by fifths in m3 set.

Linking this motion by fifths to the passage in question, we see the continuation of motion by fifths in the bass motion from $D^\flat$ in example 5.6:

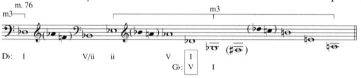

Example 5.6. Continuation of fifth motion within m3 set.

The final appearance of the m3 set in the structural coda, measures 129–32, provides the rationale for its previous incompleteness: this is the triumphant realization of the full set itself and the emotional climax of group A, beautifully summed up in the diminished chord in measure 132, which contains all the members of the m3 set and is, at the same time, the ♯IV of the key of G. Example 5.7 shows the passage as well as a schematic of its bass motion by fifths—which, in measure 131, Chopin releases in five consecutive ascents through the sharp side of the circle of fifths.

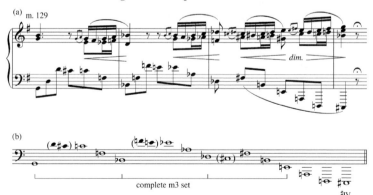

Example 5.7. Realization of m3 set and climax of group A.

The fact that Chopin *saved* the completion of the m3 set until the very end of the piece speaks to his great tactical skill as a composer: he knew what to hold back to the very last in order to prevent the work from closing down its energies too soon, saying in effect: you will understand this piece only when you have heard its last notes, and not before.

The structural layout (see ex. 5.4) makes clear that Chopin has an entirely different approach to the use of the M3 set, which is essentially locked into the very substance of the musical idea of thematic group B. Since paired members of two different M3 sets are separated by a transition within what I have designated as B/B^1 and B^2/B^3, we need to examine the key relationships of these pairs more closely to see how Chopin distributes the members of these incomplete M3 sets.

Chopin pairs members, all in major, of two different M3 sets, and alternates them: C–E; B♭–D; E–G♯; D–F♯. When related pairs are joined, complete sets result: C–E/E–G♯; B♭–D/D–F♯. The challenge is to work out intervening transitions and group A alternations while maintaining interest. The transition between the first and second pairs in B and B^1, respectively, is a freely extended, chromaticized intensification between E major (m. 42) and F^7 (V^7, m. 52), which is preparation for B♭ (I). The heightened, chromatic emotionalism of the transition makes perfect sense coming between two tranquil, becalmed diatonic areas. The keys of these areas, adjoining but separated by a transition, are a tritone apart. After an alternating group A^1, M3 set pairs return and repeat almost exactly the design of the first two pairs: E–G♯–transition–D–F♯, this time with the tritone relation between G♯ and D. There is no way of knowing for sure whether these tritone relations between pairs of M3 sets are purposeful; but it is at least safe to speculate that at some level, more conscious than not, Chopin's obsession with the tritone between G and D♭ in group A spilled over and influenced his plan of disposition of the separated pairs of M3 set keys. The final expression of B, B^4, is in G, the home key, and it is the only time Chopin uses G to express the musical idea embodied in the M3 set. It comes after the climactic diminished chord (m. 132) and makes for a perfect resolution to the complete expression of the m3 set, which is perhaps the most unstable phrase in the entire piece.

One final matter requires our attention. If we lay out for visual inspection the roots of the keys Chopin derives from both the m3 and M3 sets, we note immediately that he has employed keys on almost every step of the chromatic scale:

Example 5.8. Chromatic collection of all keys used.

What is intriguing is that if we combine both M3 sets, that is, linearize them, we get a whole-tone hexachord embedded within two m3 sets that use only four roots in common with the M3 sets: B♭, D♮, E♮, F♯ (G♭). We find we have a total of ten pitches and that the two missing pitches, B♮ and F♮, make a tritone relation to each other. We discover that neither of these pitches serves as root of a key but that they do serve as roots of localized dominant functions—but only in group B areas: B♮ as V in measures 37, 41, 83/84, and 88; F♮ as V in measures 52/53 and 57. Surely we can speculate that a mind and ear as attuned to chromaticism as Chopin's *could have* made the conscious attempt to compose a piece whose roots, whether I or V functions, in fact expressed all the pitches of the chromatic scale. Certainly conscious was Chopin's decision to make group A as chromatic as possible to contrast sharply with group B, which must strike one as being somewhat naively and simply diatonic. In light of everything we have discussed, this Nocturne must rank as a rare and unique instance of the complete use of the fully evolved symmetrical sets.

To say that certain uses of circular sets are functional and, therefore, structural, is not the same as saying they are systematic. The distinction is an important one. Brahms's use of circular harmonic sets, which we will explore in his Opus 118 Intermezzo, is no more systematic than Chopin's, yet both are clearly functional and structural. Each finds ways to build into his music, when it serves his purpose, harmonic symmetry. The fact that I am tracing out the evolution of a transformative system of symmetrical sets within the body of tonal diatonicism is quite another matter from showing some of the remarkable instances of the contributions a Chopin or a Brahms made to that transformational evolution. Obviously, neither could have guessed what lay ahead. Neither could have foreseen his part in the transformation of the very language each had mastered into an utterly different language where chromaticism would rule—often under the very centripetal forces of symmetry they had helped keep in evolving motion, forces that tended more and more to the ultimate replacement of function and structure by system and method. Such composers would not have been prepared to give up or reduce the relatively vast melodic-harmonic resources at their command for the relatively pared-down, scaled-down palette of devices that came later in the early decades of the twentieth century and served composers well into the last quarter of the century.

The Intermezzo, Op. 118, no. 4 of Brahms is as remarkable for the fact that a M3 set is the sole structural basis of its B section as for the fact that it is a strict pitch and metric canon throughout much of the piece. Before examining the M3 set in section B (mm. 52–91) in detail, let us first take a close look at the metric-pitch canon and other important aspects of section A that lead up to the double bar at measure 52. In order to see these details in operation I have sketched them out in the schematic shown in example 5.9.

Example 5.9. Schematic of section A, mm. 1–51.

The first important thing to note is that the harmony of section A, which clothes the canon, is itself not canonic as is the harmony of section B, which becomes absolutely intrinsic to the canonic procedure until measure 91 (at which point section A[1] begins and the harmony reverts to its freer treatment to the end).

The metric canon in the A section ends with measure 16, and a new figuration begins, starting three times as a canon by inversion but ending each time quite freely in order to cadence harmonically in F major (m. 20), A♭ major (m. 24), and B major (m. 28), respectively—nodes of a never-completed m3 set. However "remote" from F minor, the home key, B major may be by conventional diatonic standards, by now we understand such remoteness quite differently. The tritone key, B major, marks the beginning of a new figuration and harmonic progression, which leads through a deceptive cadence to C (V, in m. 31) to a $D^{\flat 7}$ that is really a German sixth chord in disguise—a disguise unmasked at measure 38—and returns to the opening canonic phrase in F minor again, coming to a half-close on C (V) at measure 47. With the upbeat to measure 52, section B's harmonic canon begins.

While the harmony of sections A and A^1 changes freely—but functionally—around the metric-pitch canons, the harmony of the B section does double duty: first, it expresses a complete M3 set: $A^{\flat}$ major (mm. 52–67)–E major (mm. 67–75)–C major (mm. 75–91); and second, it expresses the set canonically in three dimensions simultaneously: pitch, meter, and register. What's more, it does these things unobtrusively; that is, one is hardly aware, if at all, that a contrapuntal device is the essential structural frame for the music. Nor is one necessarily even aware that a symmetrical M3 set is the overall structural harmonic frame as traditional harmonic progressions glide into each other without any sense of forced or arbitrary harmonic motion—so that all is mellifluousness itself. The impression is of free composition, quite the opposite of the rigor and intellectual control that guide its strict canonic structure.

The uniqueness of section B is reinforced still further by the harmonic match Brahms accomplishes between corresponding measures in the three phrases that constitute the M3 set $A^{\flat}$–E–C. $A^{\flat}$ and C are the same length, that is, 16 measures, whereas E is half that length. Example 5.10 shows both the corresponding diatonic progressions of the M3 set—what I have called the harmonic match—and the length of the three phrases relative to each other.

Example 5.10. Harmonic chart showing corresponding diatonic progressions of M3 set.

Example 5.10. Harmonic chart showing corresponding diatonic progressions of M3 set—*(concluded)*

This is an intellectual tour de force of the highest order accomplished with utmost beauty and sensitivity that brings together first, a harmonic canon, which reflects at another level the metric-pitch canon of section A; second, progressions based on functional harmony that demonstrate their source in asymmetrical diatonic tonality; and finally, a virtually perfect harmonic match between the three phrases that fill out the frame of the structurally functional M3 set.

One final point needs to be made: by placing the M3 set where he does and in the particular order of A♭–E–C, Brahms shrewdly takes advantage of the final member of the set, which he has treated as I through measures 75–91, and converts it to V in F, thus reasserting its dominant function. From the upbeat to measure 92, he makes his return to F minor at the emotionally heightened level of *f*, simultaneously returning to the canonic procedure of section A, carrying it out in the concluding A¹ section of the piece as rigorously as harmonic circumstances permit.

Brahms's marrying of traditional harmonic functionality to the symmetrically limiting structural frame of a circular set reminds us of Chopin's similar treatment of these same functions in his Nocturne in G Major— the one traditional and deeply rooted in past practice, the other wholly new and unconventional, pointing ahead to future practices that would dispense entirely with diatonic functions. Now we will observe how Tchaikovsky handles both functions, using much the same approach.

There can be no doubt that Tchaikovsky is one of the great masters of tonal harmony. His harmonic palette ranges from the purest diatonicism to the most nerve-wracking chromaticism. Within this wide spectrum he ventures freely into the symmetries of functional circular sets. We will discuss Tchaikovsky's structural use of a circular set to define the thematic-formal layout—which are one and the same in this case—of the scherzo of his Fourth Symphony ("Pizzicato ostinato"). The clarity of Tchaikovsky's thought processes is as evident in his handling of orchestral color as it is in his handling of the circular harmonic set—and both are built into his thematic-formal layout.

The "Pizzicato ostinato" is based structurally on a M3 set, its three thematic sections, different in spirit and character, appearing in the order of the augmented triad F–A–D♭. Each of these nodal points is the root of a major key. However, even though in a more traditional sense it could be argued that F major is the home key of the movement, there are equally substantial reasons for claiming this is a mere convention of too-easy thinking and that, in fact, there is no "home key" but rather a complex of tonal centers that Tchaikovsky plays with quite freely, passing rapidly from one to the other without benefit of modulation (except in two instances). We should seriously consider that what we are dealing with here is what can only be called *multiple tonality* or a *tonal field*.

In example 5.11 we see the basic elements of the three thematic groups.

Example 5.11. Tchaikovsky, Symphony No. 4, Scherzo: "Pizzicato ostinato," thematic groups A, B, and C.

What is of particular interest is that the music of this movement is primarily of a diatonic cast, colored with traditional nonsymmetrical surface chromaticism, despite outlining symmetrical sets at a deeper level. In thematic group A, for example, this kind of nonsymmetrical chromaticism occurs at measure 17 with the violas and is passed on to the cellos and double basses at measure 25; it occurs again at measure 49 with the tutti strings and is followed by hocket-like figures starting at measure 57; and it occurs a third time in what could be described as the coda or closing section starting at measures 90/91 and continuing to measure 132. But for the altered chords that serve to join thematic groups A and B and thematic groups B and C (see mm. 134–36 and 169–76), the movement is singularly unchromatic—except that what controls the diatonicism of the movement itself is the chromatic symmetry of the M3 set F–A–D♭.

Starting from measure 185, the free motion back and forth between F major, A major, and D♭ major begins in earnest. At measure 185 Tchaikovsky introduces the main tune of thematic group B in its associated key of A major.

Example 5.12. Combination of thematic groups A and B.

The way the clarinet and the key of A major burst in upon the brass and the key of D♭ major is totally unexpected and wonderfully refreshing—as is the first woodwind reference to the string pizzicato motif in measure 198 following the piccolo solo in D♭.

Example 5.13. Woodwind reference to pizzicato motif of strings.

From measure 206 to the beginning of the reprise of thematic group A at measure 218 the music alternates rapidly between ideas of thematic groups B and A in two of the three keys of the set, D♭ and F.

Example 5.14. Rapid alternations between thematic groups and keys.

From the point of entry of the brass with thematic group C in measure 170, the score indicates quite clearly what Tchaikovsky is thinking as far as keys are concerned: despite the fact that the brass are playing in D♭ major, and the tenor and bass trombones have the key signature of D♭ written at the head of their respective staves, when the piccolo enters in measure 191 and is playing *in* D♭, its staff has the signature of A major at its head. Similarly, when the rest of the winds come in at measure 198 playing in D♭ major, their respective staves (with the exception of the A clarinet) have three sharps at their heads. And when, at measure 209, after a long silence, the strings reenter playing in D♭, their staves bear the key signature of A major. Only at the point of the reprise (m. 218) is the key signature of F major reinstated and that of A major canceled.

Once he has entered the key of A major at measure 133, Tchaikovsky retains the key signature for winds and strings even though it necessitates many accidentals and cancellations when he writes for winds or strings in D♭ or F. Thus, even though he does not write anything to sound in A major after the interruption by the clarinet of the brass playing in D♭ major, he continues to write the actual score as though it were still in A major—until he reaches the F major of the reprise, at which point he changes key signatures. Clearly, then, Tchaikovsky is thinking in the three tonal areas at all times—even when one or two of them are not actually sounding. This lends considerable support to my idea of a tonal field and credence to abandoning—at least for such a movement—the notion of a strict monotonality.

As the movement advances toward its conclusion, ideas are tossed back and forth with increasing rapidity. From measure 349 on, antiphonal responses between winds in F and strings in D♭ take place. At measure 357 the exchange shifts to A major and F major. Thematic group B enters in a variant form at measure 365 but in F major, growing in intensity over a long C pedal until at measure 387 it reaches F major (I). From measure 399 to the end the brass reenter in D♭, the strings and winds interrupt, at measure 407 the brass go to F, alternating with strings in F—and a final arpeggiated flourish from the strings brings the movement to its close.

What is the role of C, or E, or A♭? Except for the long pedal on C from measures 365 through 387, the answer must be: negligible. Dominant functions are present, of course, but only as local, harmonic functions. No melodic ideas appear in any dominant chord area. This harmonic reality considerably weakens the case for monotonality—certainly as applied to this movement—and strengthens the case for considering the use of a M3 set in this fashion as working in a multiple tonal field where the three keys must be granted equal structural, and therefore functional, value.

Part Three

Pitch Organization on Larger Scales

Chapter Six

The Harmonic Envelope

Symmetry leads to *self-enclosure* by rotating limited sets of pitches. In turn, self-enclosure leads to *harmonic identity* by producing what is heard as a perceptual unit arising out of the aggregate collectivity of musical sound actions. And in turn once again, harmonic identity, understood perceptually as an *aural container*, leads to what I shall call a *tonal locus*—using "tonal" here to mean something sounding, therefore a *sound-place*—which can be an element or aspect, more precisely a harmony or chord, of key-centered music; or it can be a group of elements or aspects—chords, scales (partial and complete)—from the borderland region of the tonally vague or amorphous or from free or ordered atonality.

This complex of terms is needed to describe musical processes in both traditional and more recent repertoire for which the old terminology is inadequate. With their help, we can expand the range of discussion to include altogether different approaches to the uses of diatonicism, diatonically controlled chromaticism, and symmetrical chromaticism. At the same time they will help us to enlarge our conceptual approach to what is normally considered to include harmonic function and its relation to structure. Once symmetrical chromaticism evolves, developing from embryonic stages to full maturity in the first fifty years or more of the nineteenth century, harmonic function and its relation to structure alter radically, making it quite impossible to describe chromatic behavior accurately and meaningfully with the limited terminology of diatonic monotonality.

Self-enclosure is not a precondition or premise of symmetrical operations: it is an end product of the rotation of limited sets of pitches governed by symmetrical sets. The concept of self-enclosure moves in parallel with the aural perception of new types of harmonic identity beyond simple major and minor triads, tonics and dominants, altered chords, deceptive cadences, and so on. Harmonic identity as a perceptually unified aural container is less a matter of individual chord or harmonic progression recognition than it is a matter of becoming aware of a total gestalt or sound quality that arises from patterns of pitch organization. Such patterns as heard, identifiable configurations are what I call tonal loci or sound-places—terms that may include, as we shall soon see, functional areas of key-centered tonality, but that also include types of pitch relations no longer describable by reference to tonal harmonic functions defined only by key centers.

The first of these self-enclosed, aurally contained, tonal loci is what I shall call the *harmonic envelope*. It is no small paradox that the harmonic envelope is generally not chromatic but diatonic. The paradox comes from the fact that the concept of the harmonic envelope arises in the first place—along with its companion concepts of self-enclosure, harmonic identity, aural container, and tonal locus—from my attempts to describe the operations of symmetrical sets that are large, functional, and structural. As it turns out, all these concepts apply equally well to the single diatonic harmony or chord, not necessarily expressed as a chord per se, but as melodic or accompanimental figures and figurations that add up to the aural perception of the harmony or chord that is the envelope—the perceptual container—of the passages. Harmonic envelopes occur with the greatest frequency in nineteenth-century music.

The harmonic envelope usually found in tonally functional contexts is the smallest self-enclosed harmonic unit of the three categories of tonal loci we shall be dealing with in part 3. In this context, "smallest" refers to the number of potential harmonic elements involved. Because it is the smallest, it is also, therefore, the most readily grasped aural container. This is true even when pitches other than the few that actually make up the harmony, say the C–E–G of a C major triad, move freely through the field of the triad in the form of passing notes, neighbor notes, appoggiaturas, etc. A harmonic envelope may contain all the pitches of the scales, diatonic and chromatic, that connect the individual pitches of the chord of the envelope without altering significantly the aural perception that it is *that* chord and no other that is the self-enclosed field of action and perception. From Beethoven on, the harmonic envelope takes on greater and greater presence as tonal gestures expand in structural and durational proportions. One need only think of the opening harmonic envelope of Beethoven's Ninth Symphony to see immediately what I am talking about.

Long before tonality established itself in unequivocal terms, the principle of figuration and its patterns was developed. This can be observed in the keyboard music of the Elizabethans and other composers of the early Baroque, such as Antonio Cabezón and Frescobaldi, continuing through the eighteenth and nineteenth centuries. Patterned figuration reaches its height in Beethoven, Chopin, Liszt, and Schumann, with the invention of fluid contours that activate harmony, releasing it from both chordal style and part-writing, which tend to stratify and limit the action of voices. One of the true glories of nineteenth-century keyboard music is the development of beautifully made accompanimental figures. The following examples show the harmonic envelope developed through shapely patterned figuration.

Example 6.1. Chopin, Prelude, Op. 28, no. 3.

Example 6.2. Chopin, Prelude, Op. 28, no. 5.

Nonchord tones abound but never obscure the clarity of the harmony intended.

In the following instances from Beethoven the harmonic envelope takes on strong structural function: in the first instance, the envelope serves as a powerful climax of the Scherzo of the String Quartet in F Major, Op. 135, covering a span of 47 measures; in the second (not shown), the harmonic envelope is one of the chief methods by which Beethoven accomplishes the development section of the opening movement of his Symphony No. 6, Op. 68.

Example 6.3. Beethoven, String Quartet, Op. 135, second movement.

There is an almost barbaric ferocity released in this passage. Its very obsessiveness could not have been accomplished with any harmonic clarity, considering its incredibly intense emotional pitch, unless Beethoven had had at his disposal the option of the harmonic envelope, a device he launched almost single-handedly into the compositional practice of the last three quarters of the nineteenth century. Every note of the A major scale is sounded. In the portion of the full passage shown in example 6.3, the first violin outlines the full A major chord, then descends back to A from its fifth, E, stepwise. The sixth and seventh degrees, F♯ and G♯, are the sole property of the unison figure played by the second violin, viola, and cello, which keep their registral distance from the first violin. The speed of the music is such as to set up a virtual clamor with no pitch truly distinguishable, the total effect being one that belies the utterly bland look of the music on the page.

Measures 151 to 236 from the first movement of the "Pastoral" Symphony (not shown) contain two pairs of harmonic envelopes: the first pair, a major third apart—twelve measures of B♭ major (mm. 151–62) followed directly by twenty-eight measures of D major (mm. 163–90)—is matched by a second pair of envelopes a minor third apart—G major (mm. 197–208) followed directly by E major (mm. 209–36). Far from being mere mindless padding, not-knowing-what-else-to-do harmonic mill-treading, these envelopes have their rhythmic, therefore gestural, source in an earlier two-chord envelope, a kind of harmonic stasis that Beethoven settles into from measure 16 through measure 24 almost immediately following the motto-like tune that opens the symphony. These two pairs of M3 and m3 harmonic envelopes serve large-spanned gestural, structural, and tonal functions simultaneously, allowing the inner world of the development section plenty of space through which to project its energies unhurriedly, yet directionally and purposefully.

Mahler inherited from Beethoven a strong propensity to work with the harmonic envelope, which allowed him the freedom to organize large gestures, often amounting to entire statements or sections, in such a way that all the details of motivic presentation and polyphonic combination are subsumed under an essential harmonic frame. One of the best examples is the opening of his Symphony No. 9, from measures 1 to 26, just before the change of key signature to D minor. All the elements—rhythmic, motivic, and timbral—seem, despite brief deviations touching the dominant, to float freely in the suspended harmonic space of the D major (I) envelope. Perhaps the impulse behind the late nineteenth-century development of the harmonic envelope came from a felt need to free music from its stratification into specific parts or voices without relinquishing the control and perceptual order of harmony itself.

The end of "Der Abschied" from *Das Lied von der Erde* is one of Mahler's most beautiful uses of the harmonic envelope. From rehearsal number 66 to the last note, a total of 41 measures, everything—voice and orchestral instruments—floats in the rarefied space of a harmonic envelope I am loathe to call "C major"—although there is certainly evidence for it. Still, if it is "C major," it is unlike any previous C major envelope one could point to. Every pitch of the C major scale but F is sounded—and emphasis is especially placed on the sixth and seventh degrees, A and B, until near the end, when even B is dropped. We gradually become aware that this "C major" harmonic envelope is a six-note envelope. Once that awareness rises to the surface, another slowly dawns: even granting the *ppp* three-trombone C major triad that occurs frequently, an overwhelming sense of a pentatonic presence emerges. Consequently, D–E–G–A–B (the pentatonic scale we hear) make up a secondary envelope—a pentatonic envelope based on G—sounding within the space of the primary C major envelope rooted in the trombones.

While thus far I have emphasized the essentially diatonic nature of the harmonic envelope chiefly because it developed within tonal practice, clearly any collection of pitches that produces a perceptually clear aural container can function as a harmonic envelope. To demonstrate this extension of the harmonic envelope, I conclude this discussion with a seventeen-measure passage from my sextet, *Serenata d'estate*, a work written in 1955 (ex. 6.4). Within this passage there are four successive chromatic envelopes, each deriving from a twelve-tone row in part or in whole.

Example 6.4. Rochberg, *Serenata d'estate*. © 1963 Universal Music Corp. © renewed. All rights reserved. Reproduced with permission from Hal Leonard Corporation.

Example 6.4. Rochberg, *Serenata d'estate.* © 1963 Universal Music Corp. © renewed. All rights reserved. Reproduced with permission from Hal Leonard Corporation—*(continued)*

Example 6.4. Rochberg, *Serenata d'estate.* © 1963 Universal Music Corp. © renewed. All rights reserved. Reproduced with permission from Hal Leonard Corporation—*(concluded)*

From these successive chromatic envelopes I derive four hexachords.

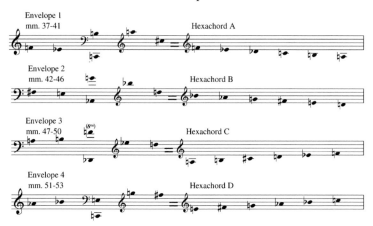

Example 6.5. Hexachordal structure of envelopes.

Each of the four hexachords in example 6.5 represents an identifiably different harmonic envelope. Envelopes 1 and 2 make up one pair, envelopes 3 and 4, the other. Hexachords A and B are retrograde inverted versions of the scalar forms each envelope reduces to. The same holds true for hexachords C and D. Once envelope 2, based on hexachord B, is established by the harp, guitar, and flute, a very soft, light figure played by the violin floats through its space. This figure is a melodic expression of hexachord A. Envelope 2, then, briefly encompasses all twelve pitches, but the envelope itself remains the tonal locus established by hexachord B. Structurally, the same thing happens in envelope 4: once the guitar, harp, and flute have established the envelope, this one based on hexachord D, the viola enters very quietly playing a figure based on hexachord C; for the two measures (52–53) that the viola plays, it floats through the space of envelope 4, filling that space with twelve pitches, without altering the tonal locus, the essential frame of the envelope. The symmetrical relationships between the pairs of harmonic envelopes bind all four hexachords on which they are based into a macro-chromatic structure that is subdivisible into clear aural containers.

At the core, then, of the harmonic envelope—diatonic or chromatic, asymmetrical or symmetrical—is the necessity for clarity of aural perception: one must be able to hear an essentially single harmonic background—a chord, a collection of related pitches, and so on. In another sense, the harmonic envelope is an idealization. That is to say, the harmonic envelope is more than the actual sounds it contains, even though it is produced by them. It is certainly more than a simple prolongation, since it is simultaneously an aural container and an often highly inflected complex of musical actions. The idea of prolongation is abstract, intellectual; it stresses the analytic summation of structural functions and tendencies of harmonic progressions rather than the psychological sensation, the gestalt of the harmonic envelope in the ear. First comes the perceptual awareness; then comes the syntactical and structural understanding.

The harmonic envelope contains melodic motion but is not limited by factors of temporal duration or the nature of melodic motion. The envelope may be nothing more than a single chord expressed through patterned arpeggiation within the limits of a measure or a few measures, or it may be larger units of temporal duration incorporating more than one chord, or still larger units embracing still more complex actions. It is a way of embracing perceptually all that is contained within a single, analytically identifiable harmonic frame of action. Ultimately we recognize the significance of the harmonic envelope in nineteenth- and twentieth-century music as a compositional device that permits the expression of long-spanned harmonic thinking that, though richly ornamented and detailed, remains fundamentally and often grandly simple, and, therefore, clear.

Chapter Seven

The Harmonic Field

In studying the major characteristics of the harmonic field I want to begin with a comparison between a harmonic field and a harmonic progression in a strangely coincidental use of the same set of seven pitches by Stravinsky and Brahms. It will illuminate the difference between a harmonic field and a harmonic progression, especially in those rare instances where they share identical pitch contents.

Example 7.1. Brahms, Symphony No. 3, second movement.

Example 7.2. Stravinsky, *Symphony in Three Movements*, first movement. © 1946 by Ernst Eulenburg & Co. GmbH. © renewed. All rights reserved. Reproduced with permission from European American Music Distributors, LLC, sole US and Canadian agent for Ernst Eulenburg & Co. GmbH.

The seven pitches on which both the second movement of Brahms's Third Symphony (mm. 57–59) and the first movement of Stravinsky's *Symphony in Three Movements* are built are: $C^\natural$–$C^\sharp$–$E^\flat$–$E^\natural$–$G^\natural$–$A^\natural$–$B^\flat$. From these pitches we derive three major triads, C, $E^\flat$, and A or their three dominant seventh forms, C^7, $E^{\flat 7}$, and A^7. The Brahms passage is clearly a harmonic progression whose larger motion involves a symmetrical m3 progression from C^7 to A^7 followed by a motion to D^7, which leads in turn to a variant form of the main theme of the movement in the dominant, G. In this passage, Brahms, of course, is still thinking in terms of harmonic progression, whether the harmony used involves symmetrical or asymmetrical connections. The nature of harmonic progression is primarily directional, a directionality dependent on carrying all melodic ideas forward and linking them through tonal functions. Tied to such conditions are phrase periodicities and their corresponding metric-rhythmic periodicities, which are the carriers of melodic-harmonic ideas and progressions.

By contrast, a harmonic field—in this case, the Stravinsky passage—stands as an independent unit of musical action, virtually self-sufficient even when it is only a single unit among others in a successive series of musical actions making up either a section, a movement, or a whole work. Its self-sufficiency begins with its tendency toward self-enclosure of pitch material, often but not always symmetrical. In that tendency lies its capacity for self-limitation. This is confirmed by the fact that virtually all identifiable harmonic fields in twentieth-century music limit themselves to a set of pitches fewer than 12.

Like the harmonic envelope, the harmonic field is an aural container, but it is much more perceptually complex. The reason is simple enough: the harmonic envelope is primarily framed within the structure of a single chord or harmony, whereas the harmonic field often contains a number of chords of equivalent status in relation to each other. While it would be rare to find them in nineteenth-century literature, by the early decades of the twentieth century harmonic fields were relatively common.

More often than not, the harmonic field is highly chromatic, though the concept of the field could be stretched to include modal and diatonic music. Because it is generally chromatic, the tonal locus produced by the field is unidentifiable by naming a chord or a key center, but can, under most conditions, be heard as a *Klang*, which is a particular kind of sound, possessing its own color, even texture, in the sense of smooth or rough, soft to the ear or hard to the ear, etc. In the harmonic field heard as tonal locus, the *Klang* replaces the ideas of "chord" or "harmony" or "chord progression" with the idea of a sound-space with identifiable relations among the pitches that collectively produce the *Klang*. These relations can be heard, for instance, in harmonic fields that result from nontonal uses of symmetrical sets that have their origins in tonality. The particular *Klang* of many of the pieces from Bartók's *Mikrokosmos*, for example, results from the constant sounding of a limited set of pitches, often in scalar, rather than chordal, form. And we could make the claim (without, however, pressing it too far) that Debussy invented *Klang* when he began to use the whole-tone scale.

The *Klang* character of the Stravinsky harmonic field (ex. 7.2) saturates it, not only with respect to pitch content but timbral content as well. One confirms the other. Harmonic fields tend to insist, via *Klang*, on their unique presence and identity. Self-enclosure of pitch content becomes a structural necessity in harmonic fields—again, a marked contrast with the harmonic progression, which is a motion from one harmonic position to others. Even where m3 and M3 progressions occur, as they do in nineteenth-century tonal music, their "from→to" motions remain. Such passages are, however, clearly a stage—when stripped of their tonal sources or uses—toward the static, nonharmonically progressing, self-sufficient harmonic field that developed around the turn of the century and came to full flower in the first half of the twentieth century.

Clearly one or more stages lie between the harmonic progression of functional tonality and the full emergence of the harmonic field. It is not conceivable that composers went from one to the other without preparation. I do not believe that that is how things happen, either in nature or in people—whether we speak of sudden and violent storms in the natural world or violent and abrupt changes in the political and social life of humans. The seeds of change lie buried deep and often work invisibly, at their own pace, until they have developed enough strength to release the transforming energy that is required to make change possible. This process is at the root of the great transformation from the nineteenth century to the twentieth century that I have been trying to describe, which led to the full-blown emergence of symmetry and its many manifestations, among them the harmonic field.

We need to find a music between Brahms and Stravinsky that is not completely free of harmonic progression yet already has some of the characteristics of the harmonic field, particularly its tendency to self-enclosed pitch sets and perceptually identifiable *Klang*. We must be able to *hear*, if not yet identify, the sonic elements that permeate and saturate the musical actions in order to make even the simplest intuitive approach to the sense that a field is operative—embryonically, if not more fully advanced. That music, I believe, can be found in the late works of Scriabin, particularly the piano sonatas of 1911 to 1913.

The opening measures of Scriabin's Sonata No. 6, Op. 62, composed in 1911, provide an example of this transitory stage.

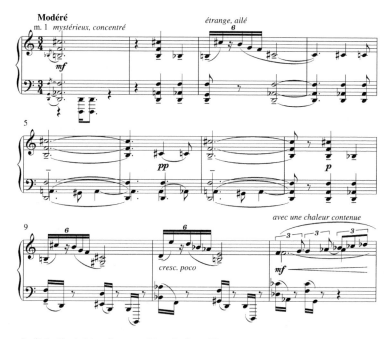

Example 7.3. Scriabin, Sonata No. 6, Op. 62.

The pitches A and C enjoy a special status in this piece: they are "foreign" to the circular harmonic set on which this work is based and, therefore, are "nonchord" tones in the context of an incipient harmonic field. The pitches on which this passage is based, laid out step-wise, produce the following octatonic scale:

Example 7.4. The octatonic basis.

A and C are excluded from this collection, as are D♯/E♭ and F♯/G♭, which are therefore also "nonchord" tones.

A special distinction of the octatonic scale is that it is perceptible without aid of structural rationale. We can hear it, even identify its *Klang*—very much as we can hear and identify, intuitively, basic tonal progressions (I–V–I; I–IV–V–I; etc.) as well as, for example, whole-tone music. This aural identity, however specific and recognizable, is severely limited (perhaps, or possibly, the very reason for its clarity and identity) and circumscribed by the narrow range of combinations available with its principal eight-note envelope to which, of course, may be added, for compositional purposes, the excluded four-note "nonchord" tones. It remains "tonal"; but the concept of monotonality or single, so-called organically determined, key is not applicable here. There is no I; neither is there a V. The chords have an equality of function and share in a kind of harmonic oligarchy. Order still prevails. There are still roots of chords; inversions of the same chords are still possible, etc. But now there is the possibility of new chords arising out of superimposition or recombination. That is, elements of one chord may become associated with elements of another chord. Therefore, roots, inversions, and chords still exist, but no longer in the sense of "functional harmony" as that concept is understood in the monotonal harmonic hierarchy. These roots, inversions, and chords have now formed a closed symmetrical system that was born in tonal function, matured within the structural order of tonality, and ultimately became independent of the old order of tonal function, existing in and for itself.

In the opening of Scriabin's Sonata No. 6, we cannot yet speak of a harmonic field as we can in relation to the passage from Stravinsky's *Symphony in Three Movements*. There is just enough of harmonic progression—even granting its clearly symmetrical character—in measures 9 to 11 to neutralize the possibility of the passage's being described as a harmonic field. Yet the first eight measures possess strong field-like qualities: the pitch content is very limited, only seven pitches of the octatonic scale being used (E♮ appears only in m. 10), plus two nonchord tones, A♮ and C♮, making nine pitches in all; there is voice-leading, but only by semitones, and therefore harmonic progression is limited only to those chord changes that half-step motions make possible. There is incipient *Klang* as a consequence of everything already described, and an approach, therefore, to self-enclosure and self-sufficiency, but measure 9 breaks that off abruptly. We feel that we are literally observing the process of change from one state to another, but it never quite frees itself from its old state, nor does it quite achieve its new state. It appears to be in its chrysalis stage: on its way, but not yet arrived. We are present, with Scriabin's music, at a stage of metamorphosis.

With our next examples, we are solidly in the achieved, arrived state of the twentieth-century harmonic field. Béla Bartók's *Sonata for Two Pianos and Percussion* makes marvelously effective use of canonic imitation organized symmetrically. At the same time, all the characteristics we associate with the harmonic field are also present: self-enclosure, self-sufficiency, and perceptual identity via *Klang*.

Example 7.5. Bartók, *Sonata for Two Pianos and Percussion*, first movement, mm. 417–20. © Copyright 1942 by Hawkes & Son (London), Ltd. Reproduced with permission.

Piano II has two canonic entries a minor third apart. Piano I follows with its pair of canonic entries also a minor third apart. The points of entry outline a diminished chord.

The resultant *Klang* of all four parts sounding together suggests that Bartók is unfolding a m3 symmetrical set polyphonically, the same set that informs Scriabin's Sixth Sonata and innumerable pieces of nineteenth-century music; however, in its new environment, it emerges with surprising freshness and new interest.

By verticalizing the first three notes of each canonic entry we arrive at what appear to be suggestions of dominant seventh forms:

Example 7.6. Verticalization of first three notes of canonic entries.

We note, too, that these four three-note chords are not made up of twelve different pitches, but rather only eight, the D♭–E–G–B♭ being a different ordering of the same diminished chord out of which the four-part canon springs. If we now verticalize the four initial dyads, we find harmonic results that combine major and minor thirds in the same four-part chords.

Example 7.7. Verticalization of first four dyads of canonic entries.

These internally equidistant minor sixth intervals, of course, are characteristic of the canonic melody. The cross relations of major and minor thirds in the two chords give each its harmonic piquancy and therefore contribute to the *Klang* nature of the passage that saturates it. If we combine both chords (of ex. 7.7) into an eight-note simultaneity, we have the harmonic summation of the four-part canon and the essential *Klang* of the harmonic field it produces.

Clearly Bartók realized the full implications of the symmetries he was working with—linearly and vertically, contrapuntally and harmonically—for in the passage that follows the canonic one he lays out the harmonies for the two pianos as follows:

Example 7.8. Bartók, *Sonata for Two Pianos and Percussion*, first movement, m. 436.
© Copyright 1942 by Hawkes & Son (London), Ltd. Reproduced with permission.

In measure 436, each piano sounds half of the tritone-related eight-note simultaneity in precise symmetry of intervals, from C♮ down to C♯ of Piano I (marked X), and from G♮ up to F♯ of Piano II (marked Y). In a sense, then, we can say that by reverting to the practice of time-honored polyphonic devices, Bartók, in this instance, contrapuntalized the harmonic field, and then, at measure 436, he shows us what it all means *harmonically*.

One might think that the next example from Schoenberg's String Quartet No. 1, Op. 7, is merely one of his early ventures into the device of stretto—a passion that he shared with Bartók (probably more than any of his other contemporaries)—and consequently one might overlook its harmonic field aspect entirely. The *Klang* character of this passage is particularly pungent.

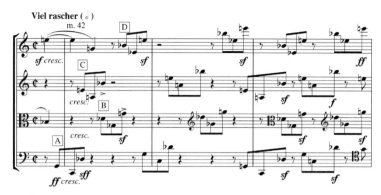

Example 7.9. Schoenberg, String Quartet No. 1, Op. 7, section C.

This stretto-like passage is based on precisely the same collection of eight pitches as the Bartók example. It comprises four three-note combinations, marked A, B, C, and D. Each trichord is made up of a fifth and a tritone. Each pitch that forms the tritone intersects with a note that is different from the one to which it is linked in the stretto to produce a series of traditional triads (shown in ex. 7.10).

Example 7.10. Production of traditional triads.

I doubt very much that one hears echoes (considering the time of the composition of this work, 1905, one should say "pre-echoes") of the "Petrouchka chord" in this passage. But one does become aware—after even so brief an analysis as this—that trichords A/B and C/D provide the basic pitch material for combinations of tritone-related superimpositions (or simultaneities) that form the skeletal frame of the "Petrouchka chord." To arrive at complete "Petrouchka chords," we would need to appropriate for inclusion in the A/B combination the B♭ (A♯) of trichord C and the E♮ of trichord D, and for inclusion in the C/D combination the D♭ (C♯) of trichord A and the G♮ of trichord B.

Implications of possible "Petrouchka chords" aside, this Schoenberg passage becomes a harmonic field projecting the intersection of all four trichords (A, B, C, and D). In the context of the string quartet itself, it is an isolated, uncharacteristic instance. Nevertheless, isolated and brief though it may be, it remains an example of an early twentieth-century venture into the harmonic field—even if it may not have been intended as such, as, I believe, the Bartók two-piano passages clearly were. Paradoxically, however, it was Schoenberg, as much as, if not more than, Bartók and Stravinsky, who first raised the idea of *Klangfarbenmelodie* from which comes the term *Klang* to designate the perceptually identifying color (or flavor) of the sound of the harmonic field. Schoenberg's one clearly conscious venture into purely harmonic color for its own sake, excluding virtually all other dimensions, occurs in the third movement of his Five Orchestral Pieces, Op. 16, which he called "Summer Morning by a Lake (Colors)," in which he works primarily with a single chord at the beginning of the piece. Schoenberg himself did not pursue this virtually pure *Klangfarben* approach. Other composers, however, did, and, particularly after World War II—especially in what briefly came to be known as the "Polish School"—they carried the idea to its extreme limits, excluding all musical dimensions except for color and texture, stressing cluster formations of half- and quarter-tone steps.

If the concept of *Klang* is broadened to include, say, *ethos*, that is, the spiritual essence or emotional atmosphere that, expressed musically, permeates a work, then we could say without any qualms that the first movement of Beethoven's Fifth Symphony has *Klang*, or a *certain Klang*. Other than Beethoven's way of infusing C minor with his peculiar psychic intensity, or *because* of it, this music has a pronounced and special color that is not traceable to any unique musical element or configuration per se, harmonic or otherwise, but makes itself immediately heard and felt with its opening notes. If we were to accept this, we could extend our range of examples to include, for example, Schubert's "Erlking"—for that matter, Schubert's "Serenade" and "Ave Maria," too—Mozart's G minor Symphony No. 40 (particularly its first and last movements), the openings of Brahms's First Piano Concerto and First Symphony, and so on. According to individual tastes we could devise endless lists of works where *Klang* as *ethos* saturates musical expression.

But I believe we would be confusing the issue, because unlike a piece's *Klang*, its ethos, its emotional color, doesn't depend on describable musical techniques. For it is of the essence that we understand that, starting with Beethoven and extending to Mahler, music takes on emotional intensities that go far beyond the frame of even the high styles, emotionally speaking, of Haydn and Mozart and that foster the development of the widest possible palette of harmonic vocabulary. It is *after* the language of harmony has been subjected to the pressures of extreme chromaticism and the parallel development of self-enclosed symmetry that composers rejected the high emotional intensities of the late romantic period and started over again from different attitudes—emotionally and compositionally. *Klang* becomes one of the technical ways to replace the ethos of key-centered music. The sheer heat of emotional intensity, the overwrought, near hysteria, of the late nineteenth century is cooled, just as the musical palette, that is, the very means by which composition is approached and realized, is radically reduced. All we need think of are works like *Pierrot Lunaire* of Schoenberg or *L'Histoire du soldat* of Stravinsky. The whole aesthetic, and consequently, *ethos*, of twentieth-century composition undergoes radical change and revision from what it was twenty-five, fifty, or one hundred years earlier. *Klang*—as a major characteristic of the harmonic field—is one of the inevitable and significant outcomes of symmetrical chromaticism.

Different energies, different aspects of the human psyche, come into play and are released in the early twentieth century and require their own characteristic expression. These energies focus on metric and pitch combinations never brought to the fore by eighteenth- and nineteenth-century composers—even though many of the pitch combinations lay dormant in earlier harmonic practice. The rhythmic ostinato, for example, of Stravinsky is a different energy expressed musically from the building up of large-scale periodicities of Beethoven. Its very sense of standing in place, stamping out simple or complex meters, that is, not driving or being driven forward, requires different harmonies and different uses of old harmonies. The self-enclosed *Klang* of a limited harmonic field becomes the perfect corollary to this kind of rhythmic stasis.

The opposite is also true. That is, a music in which physical (or muscular) rhythmic energies are suppressed, the metric beat (or pulse) suspended, must now depend solely on its pure sound characteristics. Such sound characteristics may still be harmonies of a kind, but not necessarily in an earlier sense. They need not relate as progressions from one point to another, those beginning and ending points that clearly articulate the phrase. Phrase and periodicity are not necessarily abandoned, but they undergo considerable change (as the examples in this chapter show). *Klang* becomes, therefore, an aural identifier, a means by which to grasp what one is hearing. Even if there is no name as such for a particular collection of pitches, if it possesses perceptual identity, we are dealing with, experiencing, *Klang*. Nineteenth-century harmonies are centrifugal, emanating from powerful energy cores. *Klang* is centripetal, seeking to become the sound essence of what it expresses symbolically. *Klang* is not a replacement for emotional intensity. *Klang* is the emergence of a new sound quality for emotional states unique to the twentieth century.

I would be leaving music too far behind and entering into the morass of the pathologies of twentieth-century psychology if I were to attempt to describe what these emotional states are that I consider peculiarly unique to the past century. Here I think some examples from other art forms are helpful. For instance, the expressionistic pain torn out of the mouth of the person on the bridge in Edvard Munch's *The Scream* is very close in spirit to the inner pain and terror of Schoenberg's *Erwartung*. At the other extreme of the emotional spectrum is the detached, cool irony of T. S. Eliot's "The Love Song of J. Alfred Prufrock," which has its counterpart in the detached irony of Stravinsky's early so-called neoclassic works. In one sense, at least, irony is a distancing of the self from the pain of direct emotional involvement and is more readily perceivable in its literary than its musical expression. In its literary form irony is recognizable in its ideational content; in its musical form irony generalizes itself into attitude. And while cubism is not necessarily ironic in its particularly odd vocabulary of newspapers, guitars, violins, and other objects of human use, it too requires intellectual detachment in order to narrow the palette of visual device and achieve multiple perspectives. Perhaps—but only perhaps—an analogy with Webern's serialism is possible here. But some may feel that Webern's highly contrapuntalized, chiseled-out small forms find a better counterpart in the objectified precisions of Paul Klee's miniaturized symbolic and fantastic visual worlds.

This is sufficient, I think, to point out the relationship of *Klang* to the wide and subtle varieties of the emotional range of twentieth-century art. To the extent that *Klang* is taken up by twentieth-century composers as a characteristic device, we also find that perceptual identity locates itself in ways of producing harmonic fields out of limited collections of pitches. In that sense, *Klang* is to sound complexes, that is, harmonic fields, as scent is to lilies, old roses, and lilacs: an essence of the whole.

Chapter Eight

The Tonal Field

We have already gone into certain aspects and conditions that are needed for an understanding of the tonal field. For example, we went into considerable detail in chapter 5 in examining Chopin's Nocturne in G Major, Op. 37, no. 2 and Tchaikovsky's Fourth Symphony Scherzo: "Pizzicato ostinato," in which we were already dealing with primary instances of the tonal field developed to a high degree of maturation. However, we discussed the Chopin and the Tchaikovsky as though the hegemony of traditional key-centered tonality still prevailed—even though it was already undergoing radical change resulting from the use of symmetrical techniques.

Even though traditional key-centered tonality *did* prevail when these works were written, now we can see them from an entirely different perspective, one that is informed by a full consciousness of symmetrical thinking in both harmony and form building in the twentieth century. The tonal field involves the most important considerations of large-scale design, revealing the structural layout of big proportions and the coherence among the parts that make up a work's musical substance and that result in a composition whose dimensions leave one with the sense of organic unity cast in convincing structural form. This is the same problem that eighteenth- and nineteenth-century composers had to deal with. The tonal field is not necessarily an advance over earlier ways. It simply reflects the change in thinking from the asymmetrical point of view, which was the prevailing—though hardly conscious—view in the eighteenth and nineteenth centuries, to the symmetrical point of view, which largely describes the atonal and extended tonal world of the twentieth century. It is, however, clearly more inclusive, since it has absorbed tonality's earlier functions into a structural complex that, while supplanting asymmetrical functions, simultaneously incorporates them into its symmetrical workings.

The tonal field, then, is what I shall call a *constellation* of keys—using the term "keys" more in the sense of tonal loci, that is, sound-places, than traditional tonal centers. In such a constellation there are no Is or Vs; there are only relationships of essentially equal status. The tonal field is built on the model of the circular harmonic set. That is, it is a way of structuring large-proportioned works using the symmetrical division of the octave. This division takes over from the earlier asymmetry of I–V–I circle of fifths hierarchic relations in form building and, at the same time, *takes in* asymmetrical functions for subordinate uses. This is true even after harmony has become atonalized externally, and earlier tonal functions—disguised however they may be and difficult to discern at times—still find their way into the harmonic-chordal fabric. Thus the tonal field is the end result of more than two centuries—roughly from 1800 to the present—of the evolution of symmetrical thinking, first, in the increasing chromaticization of harmony, and second, in the parallel development of alternative ways of building large forms. With the tonal field, large-scale design shifts from hierarchic, key-centered relationships to relationships of equal status held together by the great frame of the constellations of the symmetrical divisions of the octave. Carrying the metaphor of the constellation a step further, we can invoke the *satellite* that orbits any main nodal point of the symmetrical octave division, following a different and secondary symmetrical pathway. We can now appreciate the misunderstandings and misreadings of earlier commentators who, when faced with symmetrical harmony and form, resorted to the use of such terms as "wandering," "roving," and "remote" keys.

Rather than retrace earlier discussions and analyses of the appearance of the tonal field in an early stage of evolution, I want to attempt a fresh analysis of the Finale, Allegro un poco maestoso, of Robert Schumann's Sonata in F♯ Minor for piano solo, which he wrote in 1835 when he was twenty-five years old. In a 1902 edition published by G. Schirmer and edited by Max Vogrich, the opus designation reads:

> Florestan und Eusebius, op. 11
> (Robert Schumann)

There is no indication whether this is Schumann's fancy or the editor's. I suspect it is more than likely Schumann's; it is certainly in character, for this is clearly the period of early romanticism's high tide.

Especially in the Finale of this sonata, there is a new-charged energy of emotional expression made manifest through intensified chromaticism and harmonic expansion through symmetry, both markedly affecting formal structure. Schumann's full-blown romanticism needs, indeed requires, a form with which to bind together the variegated musical ideas that fairly burst the seams of this movement. And he finds it by structuring his ideas on the double circularity of two m3 harmonic sets, F♯–A–C–E♭ and C♯–E–G–B♭. Obviously, the second set stands as a series of dominants to the tonics of the first set. However, I think it would be an error to conclude from this V–I relationship that that is all there is to it and that diatonicism still rules. Between the two parts of this 462-measure-long movement, powerful tritone structural connections hold. It is only at measure 397 that Schumann uses the conventional closure of a longish coda to assert the traditionally sanctioned tonic, but now in the major mode. Finally, important M3 satellite relations between particular thematic areas develop the structural connections between parts 1 and 2 still further. Schumann leaves behind the monotonality of single key I–V–I centrism and enters into the construction of a tonal field in which structural coherence is shared equally among the members and satellites of the F♯–A–C–E♭/C♯–E–G–B♭ diminished chords that organize this movement. The role of the structural dominant is still present but is now absorbed into the circularity of tonal field relations.

The considerable length of the Finale requires a schematic sketch of the overall structure. The double-paneled structure of the movement, each part of which—from measures 85 to 151 and 275 to 342, respectively—virtually mirrors the other, chiefly at the tritone, strongly suggests a "sonata-rondo" form because of the way the principal theme makes constant returns following excursions to other themes in other "key" areas. The sense of a sonata-form recapitulation is strongly associated with the return of the principal theme at measure 190 (and in the "home key" of F♯ minor) even though, as it continues, it develops essentially parallel to the ideas of part 1 at the tritone. The schematic sketch that follows in example 8.1 shows parts 1 and 2 and the concluding coda. Thematic as well as other important areas are designated as A, B, C, etc.

Example 8.1. Schumann, Finale, Sonata in F♯ Minor, schematic sketch.

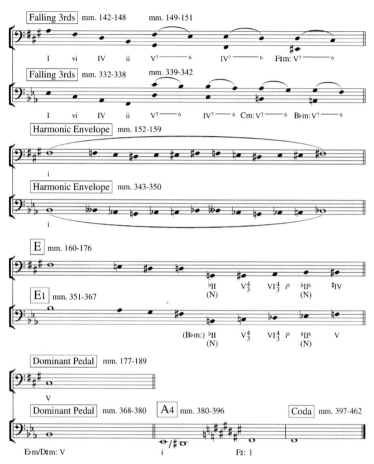

Example 8.1. Schumann, Finale, Sonata in F♯ Minor, schematic sketch—*(concluded)*

The sketch makes it possible to identify what I consider to be the principal m3 set based on F♯–A–C–E♭. Both part 1 (mm. 1–84) and part 2 (mm. 190–274) express, but in different ways, this structural diminished chord. It is at the point where both parts settle into pedals on C♯⁷ and G⁷ at [C] and [C1] that the secondary m3 set begins to emerge, controlling the relation between the parts via tritone. This produces the matching tritone, E (part 1, mm. 106–14) and B♭ (part 2, mm. 296–303 and mm. 343–80). Schumann breaks the tritone relation between parts 1 and 2 with the strangely affecting lyric idea at [E] and [E1], where the relationship is now a M3 one, between F♯ minor and B♭ minor. As previously noted, C♯, E, G, and B♭ are dominants of the principal m3 set and perhaps emerged from Schumann's thinking still in diatonic terms. Nevertheless, the end result is clearly an enlargement of the range of tonal loci toward an unfolding tonal field. Even more interesting, the two m3 sets combined as a collection of pitches produce an octatonic scale.

Though Schumann ventures deep into circular waters, there is no denying his continuing loyalty and adherence (safety measures in uncharted channels?) to traditional diatonic procedures. What is fascinating is that Schumann ventures out into chromatic waters *first*, then makes his return via the more traditional, diatonically ordered harmonic channels to close off each of the two large, almost mirroring parts, adding at the end of part 2 a substantial coda in F# major to satisfy his conventional sense of closure. We can still grant him a place among those who in the early to middle nineteenth century were laying the groundwork for the tonal field as a multicentered structure that embraced the old asymmetries of diatonicism. Schumann is neither a self-conscious pioneer nor an inventor: he is part of a generation following in the footsteps of Beethoven and Schubert and contributing to what turned out to be a multigenerational project.

What if Schumann—and his contemporaries like Chopin and Liszt, and later Brahms and Wagner—had had a premonition that let him see that the consequences of introducing symmetrical chromaticism into tonality would eventually bring about its end? Would he have pulled back? I don't think so; my guess is that he would not have, any more than Beethoven pulled back from changing sonata form; or Wagner, from changing the face of opera; or Schoenberg, from, first, inventing atonality, then subjecting it to the methodology of serialism; or Stravinsky, from "inventing" neoclassicism as a way of regaining his equilibrium after teetering on the brink of the abyss with the *Rite of Spring* and *Petrouchka*. There is no "logic" to the making of art or the impulses and energies that go into its making. There is only a kind of urgent necessity, perhaps even somewhat blind. And when a problem, direction, or tendency must be resolved, followed, or pursued, generations of composers seem to form an invisible community of mind and spirit in which they give themselves, mostly unknowingly, to furthering the evolution toward maturation.

In that sense Schumann had no more option in deciding to use the circularity of the diminished chord to organize the Finale of his F# minor Sonata than Chopin had in deciding to use both the m3 and M3 sets to organize the unique form of his G major Nocturne. Each was feeling his way intuitively toward a form—the tonal field—not to be fully realized until the twentieth century.

When a work is designated as in the key of C major or E minor or B♭ major, our normal expectations are that it will not only end in its designated key, but it will also *begin* in it. These expectations stem from the long-standing idea that a single tonality is structurally binding on a composition. It is in such a context that a certain delight and admiration develop for the composer who knows how to work *against* this "law" of organic tonal coherence and play with it, almost in mocking defiance of the "law," to produce "nontonic" beginnings. Beethoven seems to have been the master of this game, Brahms his apt pupil. The famous opening chord of the introduction to the first movement of Beethoven's C major Symphony No. 1, Op. 21—the C^7 immediately resolving to the IV chord as though the C^7 were the dominant of F—is perhaps the best known example of such a nontonic feint at the very outset of a composition.

Similarly striking, but in a totally different way, is the opening thematic idea of the fourth movement of Beethoven's String Quartet in E Minor, Op. 59, no. 2. To the casual listener it could easily give the impression of being in a major key, and this would not necessarily be wrong, for the very construction of the thematic idea is rooted in a kind of playful deception that alternates between upsetting normal expectations and quickly fulfilling them. Beethoven knew full well the "law" of organic tonal coherence and tonal centeredness, as well as the expectations flowing from them, and he deliberately set out to play *with* and *against* them.

The massive opening of Brahms's Piano Concerto in D Minor, Op. 15, announces its home key with a unison on D in horns, timpani, violas, and double basses, over which we hear, starting in measure 2, a harmonic envelope on VI^6 ($B^\flat$ major), which is followed by another harmonic envelope on V^6 (A major), which turns by degrees to i^6_4 in D minor. The entire bass motion—like a Baroque chaconne—goes by half-steps from D to A (i to V) over 26 measures, and even when we have arrived at i^6_4 in the twenty-sixth measure, we are not absolutely certain we are in the tonic per se. Brahms has indeed learned his business from Beethoven.

The point of this digression about nontonic beginnings is to introduce the very important idea that the tonal field, because it is structured as a constellation, has a binding structural law that is different from the law of tonal centeredness. Since all tonal loci in a constellation share equal relational status because they are derived from the symmetrical division of the octave, they are not bound to the conventional idea of beginning and ending in the same "key" as in tonally centered works. What nontonic beginnings show us is that composers like Beethoven, and later Brahms, were already playing with—or perhaps were impatient with—the presumed restraints laid on them by the "law" of monotonal coherence.

When we turn to Prokofiev for our first example of a twentieth-century tonal field, we find that in the last movement of his Violin Concerto No. 2 in G Minor, Op. 63 he has cast this rondo in the symmetry of a harmonic set that divides the octave by minor thirds. In so doing, he passes beyond asymmetrical tonality and single key centers into the world of the symmetrical constellation of the tonal field. The $B^\flat$ of the opening theme is not the key or tonal center of the whole movement. Rather, it is one of the three tonal loci that determine the basic symmetry of the large-scale shape of the rondo, $B^\flat$–E–G. $D^\flat$ ($C^\sharp$) has no independent thematic reference, although it is much in evidence throughout the movement. Why then does Prokofiev designate this concerto as a work in G minor with all the associations of traditional tonality that such a designation calls to mind? Is he mistaken? Or is it we who are mistaken in claiming the work answers to a totally different set of structural conditions that I have characterized as a tonal field? I believe the answer lies in recognizing that the apparent clash of states of mind with respect to "G minor"—his and our own—exists only in the appearance of the thing. We can best understand the situation if we see Prokofiev as a man of his time, still with deep ties to the culture of his youth (the nineteenth century), while engaged in vital, imaginative responses to the challenges of the time of his maturity (the twentieth). It seems to me that the most sensible way to resolve the conundrum of the "G minor" designation is to say that Prokofiev still thought in old, linguistic tonal terms, even while in reality those terms no longer applied to what he was composing.

The overall structure of the last movement is that of a classical rondo—but only with respect to the radial relationship between the main theme repetitions and the subsidiary themes: $A–B–A^1–C–A^2–B^1–A^3–$Coda. The beginning and ending "keys" answer to no traditional tonal agreement: the $B^\flat$ major and G major that begin and end this movement belong to the symmetrical set that, as I mentioned earlier, constitutes the tonal field of this piece: $B^\flat–G–E–D^\flat$ ($C^\sharp$). The heaviest thematic concentration falls on $B^\flat–E–G$ (in that order), the least on $D^\flat$ ($C^\sharp$).

Example 8.2. Prokofiev, Violin Concerto No. 2 in G Minor, Op. 63, third movement, mm. 1–10 and 25–27. © 1937 by Hawkes & Son (London), Ltd. Reproduced with permission.

Prokofiev tends, certainly in this particular movement, to show both the major and minor "faces" of "keys" without any particular emphasis on either. Like the symmetrical divisions of the octave, major and minor have taken on equivalency. For instance, in example 8.2 he shows the major-minor "faces" of B♭ in near or far juxtaposition; in example 8.3, the very design of the melody grows out of mixing the major and minor modes.

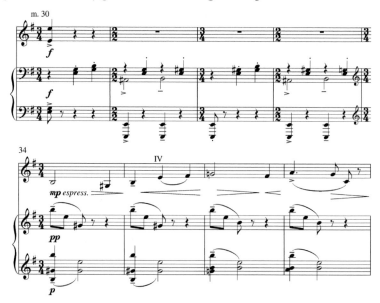

Example 8.3. Prokofiev, Violin Concerto No. 2 in G Minor, Op. 63, third movement, mm. 30–37. © 1937 by Hawkes & Son (London), Ltd. Reproduced with permission.

These equivalencies of major and minor result from two main factors: first, the breakdown of the classical-romantic ethos connecting certain kinds of emotional and spiritual states to one or the other of the modes, and in the case of some composers, to specific keys, and second, the uncontrollable growth of chromaticism in the nineteenth century, which spilled over into and inundated the twentieth in atonal and extended tonal forms. Though particular applications of harmonically mixing major and minor might differ between Schoenberg and Prokofiev, neither had need any longer for their traditional distinctions.

We turn now to the tonal field characteristics of this rondo in order to demonstrate in some detail how Prokofiev's thinking symmetrically in the large-scale successive layout of its structure is able to produce a coherent form. We will also explore why we consider such a symmetry-ruled tonal field to be a constellation no longer tied to the earth-bound gravity of a single tonal center, but a constellation with "keys" now viewed as tonal loci that are equivalent partners in a large structural relationship. In the process we will gain insight into Prokofiev's harmonic methodology, that is, how he manages to move symmetrically, yet all the while to remain in what appears, despite deviation from earlier usages, to be a diatonic language based on stepwise motion.

Let us look at the transition from the B♭ minor of measure 10 to the E minor of measure 16.

Example 8.4. Prokofiev, Violin Concerto No. 2 in G Minor, Op. 63, third movement, mm. 10–16. © 1937 by Hawkes & Son (London), Ltd. Reproduced with permission.

By stepwise and contrary motion Prokofiev leads his chords, first, to A minor (m. 12), then to E♭ minor (m. 14), and, finally, to E minor (m. 16). The tritone relation between the starting point of the passage, B♭ minor, and the ending point, E minor, is mirrored internally by the tritone relation between A minor and E♭ minor. Critical to our understanding of the harmonic motions to A minor, E♭ minor, and E minor are the roles of the connecting chords just before each "resolution": A♭ major, E$_2^4$, and A$_4^{♭6}$.

Example 8.5. Harmonic motions to A minor, E♭ minor, E minor.

A♭ and E are constituent elements of a M3 motion that, later, will be enlarged to a M3 set completed by C major. As such, these three chords will form a satellite symmetry to the primary symmetry of the movement. The harmonic devices by which Prokofiev moves in each of the progressions in example 8.5 are various—a mix of traditional and not-so-traditional progressions. The motion in (a) from A♭ major to A minor is accomplished by the presence of a common tone, C; from E$^4_2$ to E♭ minor, in (b), by the traditional resolution of a German sixth; and from A♭$^{b6}_4$ to E minor, in (c), by a M3 motion, exactly the same M3 that binds A♭ major and E major. Prokofiev's harmonic palette includes, as we have already mentioned, free mixtures of major and minor modes with the same root. Here we see an extension of that same principle applied to details of harmonic progression. We may note another interesting, albeit highly speculative, connection between A♭ major and E major and the chords of resolution, particularly A minor and E♭ minor: E major stands to A minor as dominant to tonic (V→i), and A♭ major stands to E♭ minor as tonic to altered dominant (I→v).

Having achieved E minor in measure 16, Prokofiev now embarks on two variant statements of his opening B♭ major theme, the first in E minor, the second in B♭ minor. Harmonically speaking, the movements from E minor back to B♭ major at measure 22 (ex. 8.6) and from B♭ minor again to E minor between measures 25 and 30 (ex. 8.7) prepare the way for the second thematic group, B, in E major/minor (ex. 8.3, m. 34), and at the same time establish the primary symmetry of the movement.

Example 8.6. Prokofiev, Violin Concerto No. 2 in G Minor, Op. 63, third movement, mm. 17–22. © 1937 by Hawkes & Son (London), Ltd. Reproduced with permission.

Example 8.7. Prokofiev, Violin Concerto No. 2 in G Minor, Op. 63, third movement, mm. 25–30. © 1937 by Hawkes & Son (London), Ltd. Reproduced with permission.

The constant stepwise motion of these parallel passages supports their apparent but actually deceptive diatonic appearance. In fact, each passage is based on a partial octatonic scale that, when joined together, gives us the complete octatonic motion from E♮ (m. 18) to E♮ (m. 30). These are, therefore, not diatonic but symmetrical harmonic progressions.

E minor/major is the chief characteristic of the second thematic group (mm. 34–60), B, preceded and followed by a typically Prokofievian "motto" motive also in E minor/major (see ex. 8.3, mm. 30–33). Starting at measure 64, Prokofiev introduces new secondary material that is divided into two large phrases in variant form leading to A major (m. 76) and the return of the first thematic group, A^1, at measure 83. This secondary material begins in C major, which connects back to the A♭ major/E major M3 relationship (see ex. 8.5) to form a M3 satellite set. This set is reinforced in the first of the two variant phrases when, among the many triads the solo violin arpeggiates, we find—after the C major at measure 64—E major in measures 65 and 71 and, not A♭ major, but G♯ minor, its enharmonic parallel minor, in measure 67. In the second of the two variants, C major becomes the anchor of a complete m3 satellite set that unfolds in E♭ minor, F♯ minor, and A major. This new satellite (mm. 72–75) sets up the approach Prokofiev chooses when he wishes to return to B♭ major for either subsequent repetitions and variants of the first thematic group (A^1 at m. 83; A^2 at m. 212) or the coda (at m. 338) and each time he approaches B♭ major from either A major or A minor (see mm. 76–83; 197–205; 324–38). This approach seems to be based on the principle of voice-leading by the half-step rather than on harmonic progression per se.

At measure 126, Prokofiev moves to G minor/major for his third and final thematic group, C. An important M3 shift to B major occurs at measure 159. Part of the ensuing passage introduces figurational material, which will weigh heavily in the coda. This third thematic group ends in A major and shifts again to B major, which then leads to A^2 in $B^\flat$ major. The logic of A major/B major leading to $B^\flat$ reminds us of the power of the double leading-tone, as discussed in chapter 2.

Following the A^2 thematic group, which has a considerable variation of materials, including the E minor motto figure (see m. 30, ex. 8.3), which now appears (at m. 238) in $A^\flat$ minor/major—the same M3 $A^\flat$/E satellite relationship we noted earlier—B^2 (or the second thematic group) makes its appearance in G major/minor (m. 244). At measure 270, the secondary material that originally was in C major (see m. 64) now establishes a solid D major, which acts as true dominant (V) to the preceding and following G major/minor passages. Attached to the opening measures of this dominant function on D is a new satellite circular progression: D major–$F^\sharp$ major–$A^\sharp$ minor ($B^\flat$ minor enharmonically). The next satellite comes at measure 311, a transposition of an earlier satellite passage shown in examples 8.6 and 8.7. This time the motion through the octatonic scale passes from A minor to $E^\flat$ major, then $E^\flat$ minor to A minor. The relationship between $E^\natural$–$B^\flat$–$E^\natural$ and $A^\natural$–$E^\flat$–$A^\natural$ is obviously one of fifths, but even more important, the tritones in each group, $E^\natural$/$B^\flat$ and $A^\natural$/$E^\flat$, or reversed as $B^\flat$/$E^\natural$ and $E^\flat$/$A^\natural$, bisect the octave into its two constituent tetrachords, another way of showing the symmetrical division of the octave.

Example 8.8. Dispositions of the tritones.

Both the $E^\natural$/$B^\flat$ tritone and the $B^\flat$/$E^\natural$ tritone are the symmetrical anchors of the entire movement.

We must not neglect to point out that when A^3, the final statement of the first thematic group, makes its appearance (m. 293), it is not in $B^\flat$ major, but G major, presumably tonic (I) to the large-spanned D major passage that started in measure 270 and contained the two satellites just described.

The return to $B^\flat$ major for the coda (m. 338) is short-lived, followed quickly at measure 347 by G major, from which Prokofiev does not deviate thereafter, except for the introduction and use of three satellites that encapsulate the symmetries of the tonal field, the last of which virtually summarizes the old idea of key-centered tonality combined with its symmetrical tonal locus counterpart.

Example 8.9. Prokofiev, Violin Concerto No. 2 in G Minor, Op. 63, third movement, mm. 392–95. © 1937 by Hawkes & Son (London), Ltd. Reproduced with permission.

From this mélange of superimposed, overlapping, clashing chords shown in example 8.9 we extract two satellites (see ex. 8.10): first, a M3 set made up of B major–E♭ major–G major, all three chords contained in the upbeat to measure 393 and 393 itself; and second, a m3 set (in mm. 393–95) that is the same m3 set underlying the tonal field structure of the entire movement, G major–E major–B♭ major–D♭ major (here not a complete triad, but an implication of one).

Example 8.10. M3 and m3 satellites.

The chords of the last satellite set, which are composites, superimpositions of triads or partial triads (see ex. 8.11)—C major/E♭ major, A major/E♭ major, G major/F♯ major (implied)—when reduced to their individual constituents produce the already familiar m3 circular set based on C–E♭–A–F♯, plus a G major triad (implied), which serves the function of a final tonic.

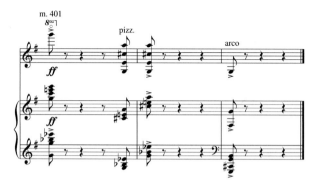

Example 8.11. Prokofiev, Violin Concerto No. 2 in G Minor, Op. 63, third movement, mm. 401–3. © 1937 by Hawkes & Son (London), Ltd. Reproduced with permission.

Since the satellite C–E♭–A–F♯ is a m3 circular set, the B♭ of the E♭ major triad can also serve as enharmonic A♯ of F♯ major, giving us four complete major triads. Whether by conscious design or not, Prokofiev has chosen the m3 set to serve as a kind of substitute dominant for G major.

Considering the four-way multidirectionality of the diminished chord in its traditional context, it seems a perfectly natural, if not inevitable, extension of the diminished chord's earlier functions to apply it on a much broader structural scale, that is, to the tonal field. This analysis also suggests that Prokofiev, believing he was still composing in the tonal tradition—regardless of the greater piquancy and dissonance of the harmonic language he employed—found in these last chord composites (whose functions are strongly analogous to old cadential functions) the right way to bring a work in G minor/major to a harmonically convincing close.

An entirely different approach to the tonal field informs the Andante tranquillo (second movement) of Béla Bartók's Violin Concerto No. 2. Bartók uses tonal field symmetry essentially for only one purpose: to mark off the beginnings of the tonal loci of the variations that make up this quite traditional—as far as the exterior form goes—theme-and-variation movement. Within the seven variations, Bartók's harmony—difficult to analyze because of heavily contrapuntalized chromatic part-writing—is essentially unnameable in conventional terms. Only in rare moments does the harmony lend itself to analytic naming. But Bartók does present us with a theme whose harmonic motion is clear, nameable, and, despite its seeming concessions to old tonal thinking, strikingly fresh in the beauty of its clear-cut phrases:

Example 8.12. Bartók, Violin Concerto No. 2, mm. 1–4. © Copyright 1941 by Hawkes & Son (London), Ltd. Reproduced with permission.

The G major tonal cast of the theme is unmistakable and is absolutely confirmed by the strong circle of fifths cadential phrase of the last two measures (10 and 11) of the theme. This cadential phrase appears four times in the work, each time harmonized differently. I am reserving a comparative chart showing all four versions until later (ex. 8.13); it will illuminate Bartók's great range of harmonic treatment, which includes both highly chromaticized aspects and traditionally diatonic step functions.

Our primary interest here is Bartók's use of a symmetrical tonal field of which the tonal loci mark off the variations. An inspection of these variations shows the following order of tonal loci: 1. G; 2. E; 3. B♮; 4. D♭; 5. B♭; 6. G; and 7. G. I am purposely avoiding designations of major and minor, because these are ambiguous throughout the movement, with the exception of the theme itself, which openly declares its locus as G major both at its beginning and its end, where it immediately joins itself to variation 1. A careful examination of structural joins—that is, where endings lead into beginnings—suggests that Bartók preferred to see each variation not as a self-enclosed unit, but as a continuously extending part of a totality. In other words, the constellation of continuously joined tonal loci takes the place of the earlier eighteenth- and nineteenth-century approach to variation structures as collections of virtually independent pieces connected only by their relation to the melodic-harmonic dimensions of the theme—and almost always in the same key, especially in the eighteenth century.

The B♮ of variation 3 is problematic in relation to the symmetry of the tonal field, which is G–E–D♭–B♭. I hesitate to call B♮ a "satellite" of E, which it follows, because it refers back to the asymmetrical dominant function and not to another symmetrical sub-field. We simply have to consider it to be anomalous until a better explanation presents itself. What is interesting, of course, is that Bartók presents variation 1 in G, the "key" of his theme. This pairing is repeated in variations 6 and 7: 7 is in one sense another statement rather than a "variation" of the theme. In any case, it is clear that the loci rotate from G to G, and there is a self-enclosing structural symmetry in the form of the movement itself. Aside from symmetrical considerations made anomalous by the B♮ of variation 3, its presence as a formal unit allows the entire movement its self-enclosing formal symmetry. Despite the I–V relation between E and B, there is no sensible way to reduce this movement to a monotonal, single-key-centered work. The rotation of G to G through the m3 symmetrical set disallows such an explanation.

I close this discussion of Bartók's work with the comparative chart I promised earlier. I offer it as a way of calling attention to Bartók's traditional roots and at the same time of loosely measuring the distance he moved away from and extended those roots through his mastery of a highly chromaticized melodic and harmonic vocabulary that embraces aspects of symmetrical thinking.

Example 8.13. Comparative chart, Bartók, Violin Concerto No. 2, mm. 8–9/10–11/124–25/126–27. © 1941 by Hawkes & Son (London), Ltd. Reproduced with permission.

The antiphonal relationship between solo violin and orchestra is amply demonstrated in these two pairs of harmonizations of the last two measures of the theme. Where they are absolutely clear and unambiguous I have indicated roots of chords (harmonic progressions). In the first pair, the altered German sixth chord, the penultimate cadential chord, resolves directly to the clear tonic, G. The route Bartók takes in the orchestral response at measures 10 and 11 is a glorious, unabashed reaffirmation of progression through the circle of fifths: from II (V/V) through the flat side to ♭II (German sixth) resolving to I. This cadential move is already more than hinted at in measure 9, where the resolution to G is embellished by ♭3–♮3.

Finally, if we compare the symmetrical organization of Bartók's tonal field to Prokofiev's, we note the direct simplicity of its structural symmetry: the tonal loci—with the exception of the B♮ locus, which breaks the symmetry and must therefore remain anomalous—rotate from G to E to D♭ to B♭ to G again, thus enclosing the structure of the movement. However, the lack of apparent, clear symmetry in the harmonic details of each variation—due largely to Bartók's penchant for polyphonic treatment of part-writing—leaves the issue of intrinsic symmetrical harmony up in the air (as far as this movement is concerned). Virtually the opposite can be said of Prokofiev. The interior harmonic details are eminently clear in their symmetrical organization and, as a consequence, prolific in their production of satellites. What is less apparent is the organization of the tonal field that enfolds these symmetries and satellites. In other words, the large-scale aspects of Bartók's tonal field are clearer than those of Prokofiev's, whereas the small-scale aspects of Prokofiev's symmetrical harmonic treatment are more obvious than Bartók's—which, if they are there, remain to be revealed.

The next two works I will discuss are compositions of my own. Each exhibits in its own way symmetrical organization of the work as a whole. The first, *Ricordanza*, for cello and piano, is, paradoxically however, a *tonal* work in its internal organization. The second, *Sonata-Aria*, also for cello and piano, is chromatically realized both in its harmonic details and overall tonal field construction. A discussion of these works will, I believe, convey a sense of the enormous variety of treatment the tonal field makes possible.

In 1972, when I wrote *Ricordanza*, I was already thoroughly familiar with the properties of circular harmonic sets and had, in fact, acquired most, if not all, of the insights into symmetrical chromaticism on which parts 1 and 2 of the present volume are based. Therefore, it is no surprise that though the melodic-harmonic language of this work is largely diatonic in its local motions, its expanded ABA structural form is enclosed essentially in the frame of a symmetrical set based on M3 arrived at through deceptive cadences rotating through A major (I)–E^7 (V)–F major (I)–C^7 (V)–D♭ major (I)–A♭^{7} (V)–A major, etc.

The first section, A, of *Ricordanza* shows a large-scale movement from A major (I) to E⁷ (V):

Example 8.14. Rochberg, *Ricordanza*, mm. 1–6 and 26–32. © 1974 by Theodore Presser Company. International copyright secured. All rights reserved. Reproduced with permission from Theodore Presser Company.

The turn to section B (see ex. 8.15) and F major occurs at measure 33. The descending diatonic melodic motion in the piano is developed in C minor (beginning at m. 52) through mediant (E♭) and fifth motions (A♭, D♭) until G♭ major is reached. G♭ major becomes F♯ major enharmonically at measure 66 and turns to B major. A tritone motion to F♮ in the cello at measure 67 returns to F major through its subdominant B♭; the B section is slowly guided to C⁷, which forms the deceptive cadence link to D♭ major and the return of section A (ex. 8.16).

Example 8.15. Rochberg, *Ricordanza*, mm. 33–38. © 1974 by Theodore Presser Company. International copyright secured. All rights reserved. Reproduced with permission from Theodore Presser Company.

Example 8.16. Rochberg, *Ricordanza*, mm. 82–91. © 1974 by Theodore Presser Company. International copyright secured. All rights reserved. Reproduced with permission from Theodore Presser Company.

The crucial turn from A♭⁷ to A major, which completes the rotation through the deceptive cadence M3 set, occurs at measures 97–98:

Example 8.17. Rochberg, *Ricordanza*, mm. 97–100. © 1974 by Theodore Presser Company. International copyright secured. All rights reserved. Reproduced with permission from Theodore Presser Company.

The work completes itself with an E⁷ preparation for a cello cadenza that ends on a V pedal, followed by a V⁷ that is built by the piano over a I pedal in fantasia style, bringing the composition to its close on the tonic A major.

In all respects the purely local melodic and harmonic motions of *Ricordanza* must be described as essentially rooted in traditional diatonic tonal practice. This, of course, is purposeful. But just as purposeful are the large-scale structural motions that frame the local diatonic details, both melodic and harmonic, within the loci of the M3 symmetrical set, which rotates through A major–F major–D♭ major–A major. The following question arises: does the symmetrical framing of local diatonicism give us the right to call such a structure a tonal field? In my view—and aside from the fact that the work lacks satellites—the work is clearly a tonal field, because of the rotation through the tonal loci of the M3 set. To ignore its symmetry in order to describe it *only* as a tonal work composed in an earlier tradition of diatonic harmonic motion is to fall into a serious analytic trap.

The *Sonata-Aria* is a work written in 1992 and exhibits a broader view of the possibilities of symmetrical structure generally and of the tonal field in particular. I would not describe it as an advance over the *Ricordanza*, but rather as a deeper exploration of the tonal field and a widening of the possible treatment of both chromaticism *and* diatonicism, for, aside from its structure as a tonal field, it is simultaneously a meditation on minor and major triads. It is far too complex and long a work to discuss in great detail here. Regretfully, therefore, I must confine my discussion only to the most pertinent aspects that illuminate its characteristics as a tonal field constellation.

The first major level of structural organization to point to is the basic m3 set, which provides the essential tonal loci of the work: two tritone-related pairs of pitches, B♭/E and G/D♭. The first pair is expressed through B♭ minor and E minor triads, the second through G major and D♭ major triads:

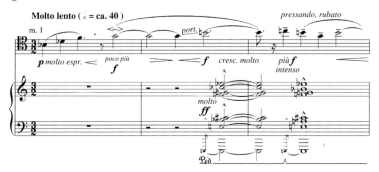

Example 8.18. Rochberg, *Sonata-Aria*, mm. 1–3. © 1994 by Theodore Presser Company. International copyright secured. All rights reserved. Reproduced with permission from Theodore Presser Company.

Example 8.19. Rochberg, *Sonata-Aria*, mm. 22–24. © 1994 by Theodore Presser Company. International copyright secured. All rights reserved. Reproduced with permission from Theodore Presser Company.

Example 8.20. Rochberg, *Sonata-Aria*, mm. 196–97. © 1994 by Theodore Presser Company. International copyright secured. All rights reserved. Reproduced with permission from Theodore Presser Company.

Example 8.21. Rochberg, *Sonata-Aria*, mm. 259–61. © 1994 by Theodore Presser Company. International copyright secured. All rights reserved. Reproduced with permission from Theodore Presser Company.

No effort is made to link these minor-major triads and the loci they establish to traditional diatonic procedures, harmonically speaking. Unlike the *Ricordanza*, which was composed through diatonic tonal practice, albeit hinged on a M3 structural symmetry, the *Sonata-Aria*—for all its references to triadic, melodic figurations, both minor and major—is a chromatic work in terms of local details (although there are, very occasionally, intended exceptions) and overall structural layout. D♭ major is represented in variant forms (not shown): first, as the locus of the second thematic group (beginning at m. 67) but spelled as C♯ major; second, as a C♯ minor locus of the final section of the work (beginning at m. 328), generated out of the minor form of the diatonic triad with which the work began and that continues as one of its main preoccupations throughout.

The second major level of this discussion concerns itself with the satellite formations, which are frequent and feature extensions of motivic ideas, both harmonically and contrapuntally. I shall give an example of each. Three pairs of measures, 92/93, 105/106, and 141/142, begin phrases of differing lengths that are developmental in nature. The loci of these three pairs express a M3 symmetrical set based on A♭–E–C.

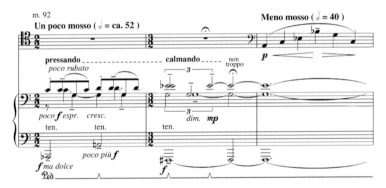

Example 8.22. Rochberg, *Sonata-Aria*, mm. 92–94. © 1994 by Theodore Presser Company. International copyright secured. All rights reserved. Reproduced with permission from Theodore Presser Company.

Example 8.23. Rochberg, *Sonata-Aria*, mm. 105–7. © 1994 by Theodore Presser Company. International copyright secured. All rights reserved. Reproduced with permission from Theodore Presser Company.

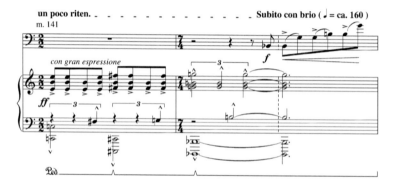

Example 8.24. Rochberg, *Sonata-Aria*, mm. 141–42. © 1994 by Theodore Presser Company. International copyright secured. All rights reserved. Reproduced with permission from Theodore Presser Company.

Possibly, one can consider such treatment as an alternative to, or analogous with, the more traditional use of fifth motions so common in eighteenth- and nineteenth-century tonal practice. The major difference, of course, between these two approaches to establishing harmonic direction is that the loci of the symmetrical set are free of the gravitational pull of a "tonic," whereas fifth motions are obviously motions away from or back to a designated, established tonic or a fundamental relation to that tonic. Such a difference is certainly not to be taken lightly, for, regardless of the method of organization, a composition is still just that: a work composed of elements in organic relation to each other such that coherence and inevitability, that is, an intuitive sense of rightness capable of being corroborated analytically, are the end result, a result that can—under optimal conditions—be substantiated by different observers.

As examples 8.22–8.24 demonstrate, the use of a M3 symmetrical set (A♭–E–C) as a satellite serves as a generator of continuing phrases in a long developmental section. Example 8.25 shows the contrapuntal use of a m3 set as a satellite generating a stretto-like passage between cello and piano. The set is based on A♭–B♮–F♮–D♮.

Example 8.25. Rochberg, *Sonata-Aria*, mm. 110–19. © 1994 by Theodore Presser Company. International copyright secured. All rights reserved. Reproduced with permission from Theodore Presser Company.

I would describe this as an *interior* satellite inasmuch as it comes between measures 105 and 141, which are the starting points of the second and last members (loci) of the M3 set A♭–E–C (see exx. 8.23 and 8.24). This ten-measure phrase begins as a series of overlapping, canonic imitations, that is, as a stretto, and ends as a series of overlapping and conjoining dominant seventh harmonies that are derived from the same diminished chord that generates the stretto. Thus, in the piano part, the right hand top voice passes through the diminished chord E♭–C♮–A♮–G♭, the pitches being the flat seventh degree of F^7, D^7, B^7, and $A^{♭7}$, respectively. The left hand uses the identical pitches and dominant seventh chords, but in a different order. The mutual confluence of these pitches and chords expresses an octatonic set.

Thus the tonal field becomes a constellation by virtue of the symmetrical order(s) of its structure, which has two essential levels: first, the structurally equal tonal loci, which are the hinges of the major ideas and sections of the work; and second, the symmetrical satellites, which flesh out the ideas of the work as variant or developmental sections. The traditional asymmetry of diatonicism is absorbed into the larger symmetrical field and may function on a variety of levels—except for the crucial one of large-scale, overall structure.

The *tonal field as constellation* is an expanded principle of large-scale structural coherence based on the symmetrical division of the octave in contradistinction to the asymmetrical division of the octave, which pulls all motions into its core center—the tonic. However, as no important device for structural organization is discarded, the almost sacred, binding concept of the tonal center is now transformed into its new guise as *tonal locus.* Nor is the harmonic character of the tonal locus necessarily predetermined by the symmetrical nature of the tonal field. It may be a harmonic envelope or a harmonic field. It may be asymmetrically diatonic, it may be symmetrically chromatic. It may also be the harmonic launching pad for a series of symmetrical satellites. All these possibilities exist. My point is that the tonal field is not just a technical device, but the evolutionary end point of at least two centuries of development of symmetrical formations from the chromaticism of the major-minor diatonic system. As such, the tonal field is the inheritor of everything valid that has contributed to the possibilities of musical expression, including the atonal experience.

The tonal field is open—and, I believe, yet to evolve, through stages still unforeseeable. We can no more close off the tonal field to further stages of morphological growth than we can close off the need for continuing musical expression—even if we do not yet know what they may bring forth. We need to be guided by the half-conscious, intuitive, inner sense that the language of music is an ever-expanding language of evolving human consciousness. In that expansion, the potential combinations of the polar opposites of symmetry and asymmetry, chromaticism and diatonicism, atonality and tonality, and tonal field and tonal center are no more anomalous than are the combinations of polar opposites in harmony and polyphony, monophonic forms and contrapuntal forms, dance forms and song forms, and major and minor modes in tonal music.

Part Four

Looking Ahead

Chapter Nine

The Shadow of Futurity

Coming to Terms with Webern's Harmony

Webern is one of the major figures of modernism who forged an intensely personal and consistent approach to ordered chromaticism that achieved a unique level of stylistic purity—so pure, in fact, that it became a veritable model for the post–World War II generations, even serving Stravinsky, whose last works were cast in the mold of the self-imposed limitations of serialism. What the early appraisals of Webern's highly charged, prismatic structures seem to have missed, however, is his stubborn insistence on creating a harmonic syntax that retained, despite its seemingly sole concentration on serial procedures, powerful aural identities even though he had presumably abandoned pre-twentieth-century tonal criteria. Now, after the death of single-vision modernism, we understand Webern's music differently. This major shift in analytic insights allows us to see Webern's harmonic search, which was incubated in the symmetries of nineteenth-century circular harmonic sets and purified in the white heat of his pursuit of the twelve-tone method, finally emerge with his *Variations for Orchestra*, Op. 30 on a plateau of organization that, paradoxically, restates the tonal sources of nineteenth-century harmonic circularity in twentieth-century atonal serialist terms. I am totally convinced that the restatement is fully intended. What I am less certain of is whether Webern understood its implications. It is impossible to know whether he intuited—however dimly—that beyond symmetrically ordered chromaticism lay a future realm of musical composition in which asymmetrical tonal forms and symmetrical atonal forms would be brought together. Whether he did or not, there was no way he could foretell the coming end of atonality any more than, say, Wagner or Brahms could foretell the coming end of tonality. The shadow of futurity lies across the path of all human actions and behavior. All we can say for certain is that Webern's realizations in the realm of harmony are among the clearest probes into the future still to unfold in the twenty-first century, in which a new fluidity between the polar opposites of diatonic, tonal asymmetry and chromatic, atonal symmetry is being established.

What then do I mean by "harmony" with reference to Webern's music? Primarily, two things: first, that "harmony" in the sense of interrelations in the pitch domain exists as aurally definable events with respect to *succession* and *progression* along a mental axis of heard connections; and second, that collections of pitches, regardless of number, cohere on the two levels that can be said to define "harmony" in all kinds of multivoiced music, regardless of style or epoch: position and movement. *Position* refers to synchronous temporal collections. *Movement* refers not only to the successive temporal unfolding of such collections, but also to the aural gathering-in of pitches expressed motivically or melodically, regardless of how they are expressed rhythmically.

In Webern's case we confront a problem common to other early twentieth-century composers: to be able to discuss in specific terms a new harmonic syntax that obscures, suspends, or suppresses aurally perceivable "tonal" centers in any traditional sense while retaining directionality; that is, it continues to make meaningful connections between pitches. Webern is perhaps one of the last acknowledged masters to insist on structural meaning in the domain of discrete pitch. After 1950, what I believe to have been the misperception of Webern helped to open the doors, along with other influences—including Varèse, electronic music, and aleatory music—to the noise spectrum and microtonal and semitonal clusters. This generalization of the pitch domain, often described as "density," implies forms of statistical saturation of the aural space that are essentially antiharmonic, because they deny discreteness, and are, therefore, antidirectional. Whatever value for composition such forms of density may have, they lie beyond the range of this discussion. One point needs to be made, however: regardless of the introduction of new devices for pitch association, "harmony" in the sense I have used above continues to exert its demands upon us, both in terms of conception and perception.

Harmonic Authenticity

The clarity and rightness of sound of Webern's music constitute not only its immediate appeal but also its mystery and authenticity. If it could be demonstrated that these qualities of clarity and rightness derive, for example, from his special ways of handling serial operations, then perhaps an explanation, in part at least, of its mystery could be managed, but not, in my view, its authenticity. For what is authentic in art is not necessarily or readily attributable to its matter or the morphology that renders that matter perceivable. So-called perfect works in which structure follows external criteria so as to relate on a "one-to-one" basis to such exterior precepts are not necessarily authentic, and authentic works are, as it turns out, often structurally flawed. But it has not yet been demonstrated that an ultimate understanding of what is actually happening in Webern's music is to be arrived at by tracing out his serial manipulations. The attempt has been made—and many times now—but it has turned out, so far, to be frustrating, if not, in fact, fruitless, because, for reasons yet unexplained and about which one can still only conjecture, serialism does not relate readily to our aural perception. Unfortunately, we work with imperfect perceptual capacities and either take in less than the object of perception offers or attribute to it more than it contains.

The problem of how to hear atonal or serial music is, amazingly enough after an entire century has passed, still very much with us. It stems, in great measure, from the fact, acknowledged or not, that starting with the atonal works of Schoenberg around 1908, no clear external referents exist for determining harmonic connections between chords or the interrelationships of motives or melodies with supporting synchronous collections of pitches. What then are the conditions or criteria that led Webern to make the choices he made? What is there about its *Klang*, the ring of Webern's music, that ultimately supersedes considerations of serial structure and separates it from the music of his contemporaries and his followers?

Clues to Understanding Webern

Webern's penchant for symmetrical construction of rows and formal compositional structure has been well established. I want to examine briefly here two instances of symmetrical construction from his mature works, both of which contain an element of surprise, analytically speaking, because one would not have expected to find the underlying organization to inhere in the balance of symmetry. In the first example, suggestive of what follows rather than complete in itself, we see Webern setting a limit to the pitch ambit and arranging his motivic cells so that their total pitch configuration lies equidistant from the axis F#/F♮. It is worth remarking here that the interval content of Webern's pitch ambit governed by the F#/F♮ axis (see ex. 9.1c) and the interval content of Contrapunctus 12 and Contrapunctus 13 from Bach's *Art of Fugue* are both based on the internal symmetry of the Dorian mode.[1] One wonders if this is pure coincidence or whether Webern, in fact, melted down the old Dorian, reconfigured its constituent elements (now completely chromaticized), and put them to new uses in a nonmodal, nontonal context.

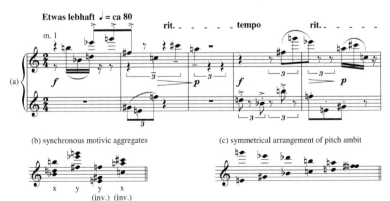

Example 9.1. Webern, Concerto, Op. 24, first movement. © 1948 by Universal Edition A. G., Wien. © renewed. All rights reserved. Reproduced with permission from European American Music Distributors, LLC, US and Canadian agent for Universal Edition A. G., Wien.

The second example, complete in itself, is even more interesting, because it organizes a seemingly free flow of chords around an axis note, E♭, which is not always explicitly stated:

Example 9.2. Webern, *Variations for Orchestra*, Op. 30, second variation. © 1956 by Universal Edition A. G., Wien. © renewed. All rights reserved. Reproduced with permission from European American Music Distributors, LLC, US and Canadian agent for Universal Edition A. G., Wien.

Given the tempo of this eighteen-measure variation, ♪ = ca. 160, the duration is less than half a minute. This makes the form of the variation perfect for its brevity: measures 1–6: statement; measures 7–8: structural fulcrum or mid-point (including m. 9, 3/8 rest); measures 10–14: retrograde of statement symmetries; measures 15–18: codetta.

Tonal Source of Webern's Harmonic Symmetry

It becomes important at this point to consider where else—other than in his twelve-tone music—we might discover this urge of Webern's toward harmonic symmetry and its closure functions. The search leads back to his earliest works, pre-Opus 1, which were written between 1899 and 1908. These are manifestly student works, albeit by a very gifted student. The clue lies in Webern's preference for mediant relations.

As we have seen, it is not uncommon to find passages in which composers move freely between the two circular harmonic sets, now invoking the augmented triad set (M3), now the diminished chord set (m3). Such an untidy procedure is perfectly normal in a period when an intuitive urge toward symmetry and closure, while beginning to assert itself, has not yet driven out the open-ended hierarchic functions of diatonic tonality completely. This is the state in which we find Webern in his early tonal music. In "Aufblick," the second of eight early songs composed between 1901 and 1904, we find the following progressions:

Example 9.3. Webern, "Aufblick." From *The Anton Webern Collection: Early Vocal Music*, by Anton von Webern, edited by Matthew R. Shaftel. © 2004 by Carl Fischer LLC. International copyright secured. All rights reserved. Reproduced with permission from Carl Fischer LLC.

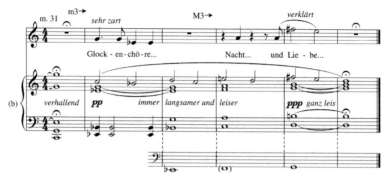

Example 9.3. Webern, "Aufblick." From *The Anton Webern Collection: Early Vocal Music*, by Anton von Webern, edited by Matthew R. Shaftel. © 2004 by Carl Fischer LLC. International copyright secured. All rights reserved. Reproduced with permission from Carl Fischer LLC—*(concluded)*

In the eighth song of the same group, "Heimgang in der Frühe," there are innumerable instances of such mixtures of circular harmonic sets. One of special interest deserves note here because the progression involves dominants with 7ths and 9ths:

Example 9.4. Webern, "Heimgang in der Frühe." From *The Anton Webern Collection: Early Vocal Music*, by Anton von Webern, edited by Matthew R. Shaftel. © 2004 by Carl Fischer LLC. International copyright secured. All rights reserved. Reproduced with permission from Carl Fischer LLC.

Particularly strong mediant functions dominate "Freunde," the last of the three *Avenarius Songs*. The climax is based entirely on major chords whose roots outline a diminished chord:

Example 9.5. Webern, "Freunde." From *The Anton Webern Collection: Early Vocal Music*, by Anton von Webern, edited by Matthew R. Shaftel. © 2004 by Carl Fischer LLC. International copyright secured. All rights reserved. Reproduced with permission from Carl Fischer LLC.

The Dissolving Agents of Tonality

As Webern develops, he sheds, reduces, and unifies. Along with the tonic-dominant function (though at times the presence of a key signature indicates he is thinking "tonally" but nevertheless suppressing the "keynote [Grundton]," as he calls it)[2] he sheds mediant relations as functional points of progression but retains the augmented triad, not as a circular set per se but as a harmonic realm. In short, by a process of reduction he casts aside the tonal form and retains its harmonic symbol, so to say. The *Dehmel Songs* reveal this process of reductionism, but it is especially clear in the String Quartet of 1905. In both there are still traces of tonics and mediant relations, but the semitones and the augmented triad are beginning to exert enormous pressure and to push aside the harmonic language of only a few years prior. The struggle for domination is clearly revealed in the Passacaglia, Op. 1, and once into Opus 3 we see Webern thinking in terms of the equalization of twelve chromatic pitches rather than the hierarchy of seven diatonic steps plus five chromatic colorations.

Having mastered the "tonal field," as *he* called it,[3] of the chromatic scale and giving the row his particular stamp, Webern closes the circle of his harmonic thinking by discovering a new way to incorporate into the chromatic field the basic elements of the old tonal functions it seemed he had left behind forever. The turning point is Opus 21. While much remains refractory and obscure, as though seen "through a glass darkly," in Opus 30, the *Variations for Orchestra*, there is one variation, the first, that shows how Webern integrates the old and the new and allows us a view of what may be at work deep below the surface. In order to carry out this limited examination, there are two practices in nineteenth-century music that need to be discussed.

The first is the combination of major and minor, which Webern himself acknowledged as one of the dissolving agents of diatonic tonality; it became one of the commonly held attitudes of harmonic ambivalence among nineteenth-century composers.[4] Whether it is the presence of a minor subdominant in a major key; or a play on both major and minor modes of a triad (as in Mahler's Sixth) or of the key itself (as in the Andante movement of the Schubert C major Symphony); or oscillation of the size of the sixth scale degree, for which Beethoven had a particular fondness—this mixture of modes expressed successively eventually found its way into synchronous forms in the twentieth century, the most common of which are these:

Example 9.6. Mixture of modes.

The second nineteenth-century practice that we need to note here is the tendency to superimpose chords of different function, one on the other, as for example:

Example 9.7. Superimposition of chords of different functions.

Probably the most famous of such combinations is the V/I passage just before the recapitulation of the "Eroica" first movement where the horn enters *pp* under violins I and II *ppp* (mm. 394–95). As chromaticism took over more and more, the forms of superimposition in nineteenth-century music became more complex, that is, harder to "hear," and their appearance more frequent. By 1911, when Schoenberg wrote his *Harmonielehre*, he was discussing superimpositions of augmented triads to form six-note chords and the possibility of deriving four dominant minor 9th structures by bringing together two diminished chords, one static, the other outlining a series of roots:

Example 9.8. Dominant minor 9ths resulting from two diminished seventh chords.

Almost at the same time, Mahler was writing combinations like this one in his Tenth Symphony:

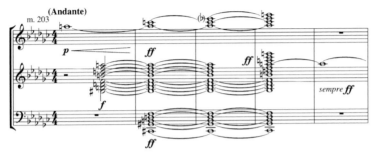

Example 9.9. Mahler, Symphony No. 10, first movement. © 1966 (renewed) by Associated Music Publishers, Inc. (BMI). International copyright secured. All rights reserved. Reproduced with permission.

And Scriabin in 1912–13 was producing multilevel chords like these in his Tenth Piano Sonata, Op. 70:

Example 9.10. Scriabin, Sonata No. 10, Op. 70.

Webern and the Tonal Imperative

Now let us return to Webern and the first variation of Opus 30. The almost naive homophony of this section masks its complexity on other levels. The clarity of its phrase structure, which is reinforced by tempo and dynamics, strengthens our sense of its traditionalism. Each phrase tableau, essentially static harmonically, links up with the next to produce a clear sense of connection and direction from the first to the last note.

Besides frequent major-minor juxtapositions, Webern makes constant use of superimpositions of tonal triadic functions, particularly V and I, vii°7 and I, and ♯iv°7 and I, this last sometimes combined with the dominant, producing in effect a triple superimposition. All of these forms, with the exception of the triple superimposition, may be readily found in Beethoven, Schubert, and Brahms. By the mid-nineteenth century they were common coin of the harmonic realm. In theory, at least, it was inevitable that all kinds of superimpositions, including the tritone triad/tonic triad, would emerge in the twentieth century. Seen in this light, Webern is not merely (or even just nostalgically) linking his harmonic thinking to earlier practice but drawing symbolic vestiges of this practice into the context of ordered chromaticism. Perhaps in some subtle way Webern is trying to say, in effect: the old lives in the new but in unexpected ways and guises.

In the four-tiered chart of example 9.11 we can trace Webern's harmony. This may be more clearly seen in the three-staff "Harmonic Progressions." In phrase 1 we observe the mixed major-minor thirds, A$\natural$/A$\flat$, in a superimposition of V and I; in phrase 3 we observe the introduction of the raised fourth degree, E$\natural$, in a complex of V and I, which intensifies to a triple superimposition of V, $\sharp$iv$^{\circ 7}$, and I; and in phrase 4 we observe a vii$^{\circ 7}$ with a I; etc. These "local" harmonic phenomena are produced by the intersections of "melodic" pitches that derive from row segments (shown in the three-staff "Row Forms") as they enter the harmonic field and combine with the closely voiced harmonies shown in the lower two staves of the three-staff "Short Score."

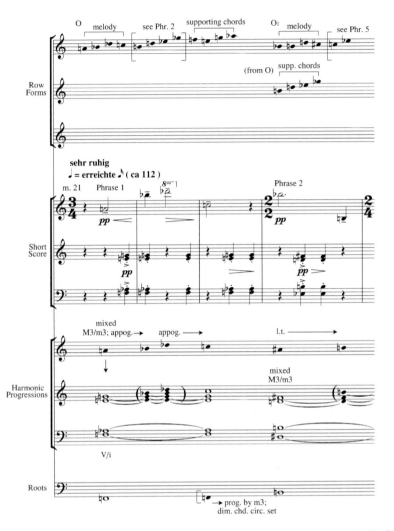

Example 9.11. Webern, *Variations for Orchestra*, Op. 30, first variation. © 1956 by Universal Edition A. G., Wien. © renewed. All rights reserved. Reproduced with permission from European American Music Distributors, LLC, US and Canadian agent for Universal Edition A. G., Wien.

Example 9.11. Webern, *Variations for Orchestra*, Op. 30, first variation. © 1956 by Universal Edition A. G., Wien. © renewed. All rights reserved. Reproduced with permission from European American Music Distributors, LLC, US and Canadian agent for Universal Edition A. G., Wien—*(continued)*

Example 9.11. Webern, *Variations for Orchestra*, Op. 30, first variation. © 1956 by Universal Edition A. G., Wien. © renewed. All rights reserved. Reproduced with permission from European American Music Distributors, LLC, US and Canadian agent for Universal Edition A. G., Wien—*(continued)*

Example 9.11. Webern, *Variations for Orchestra*, Op. 30, first variation. © 1956 by Universal Edition A. G., Wien. © renewed. All rights reserved. Reproduced with permission from European American Music Distributors, LLC, US and Canadian agent for Universal Edition A. G., Wien—*(continued)*

Example 9.11. Webern, *Variations for Orchestra*, Op. 30, first variation. © 1956 by Universal Edition A. G., Wien. © renewed. All rights reserved. Reproduced with permission from European American Music Distributors, LLC, US and Canadian agent for Universal Edition A. G., Wien—*(continued)*

Example 9.11. Webern, *Variations for Orchestra*, Op. 30, first variation. © 1956 by Universal Edition A. G., Wien. © renewed. All rights reserved. Reproduced with permission from European American Music Distributors, LLC, US and Canadian agent for Universal Edition A. G., Wien—*(continued)*

Example 9.11. Webern, *Variations for Orchestra*, Op. 30, first variation. © 1956 by Universal Edition A. G., Wien. © renewed. All rights reserved. Reproduced with permission from European American Music Distributors, LLC, US and Canadian agent for Universal Edition A. G., Wien—*(continued)*

Example 9.11. Webern, *Variations for Orchestra*, Op. 30, first variation. © 1956 by Universal Edition A. G., Wien. © renewed. All rights reserved. Reproduced with permission from European American Music Distributors, LLC, US and Canadian agent for Universal Edition A. G., Wien—*(concluded)*

The harmonic root line that we derive from this analysis contains eleven chromatic pitches. The missing root is C (V), the very one without which "tonality," in the traditional diatonic sense, could not be said to function:

Example 9.12. The harmonic root line.

The row sources indicated above the three-staff reduction in example 9.11 pale, in richness and musical meaning, in comparison to the harmonic interpretation I have offered. This is not to say that there is no meaning in Webern's employing the row as a controlling agent on one level, but rather, that the row forms apparently do not necessarily determine the choices that result in the axes of harmonic connection, direction, and continuity. Something else is guiding these axes, and I submit that it is Webern's ear operating in relation to a *tonal* imperative. Just as Schoenberg's last works paradoxically reveal marked tonal tendencies in his choice of hexachords, so Webern in his late works shows serialism transforming itself harmonically under the pressures of a new-found sense of tonal possibilities that embrace both asymmetrical diatonic and symmetrical chromatic harmonic motions. A close examination of the melodic voice-leading, of the harmonic complexes based on major-minor mixtures and on superimpositions of diatonic step functions such as V and I, and vii°[7] and I, and of Neapolitan functions, as well as of circular progressions chiefly by m3, is far more revealing of this music's meanings, I believe, than a purely serial analysis could ever be. It takes us where analysis should take us—into the ear and thought processes of the composer. We hear what the composer hears when he is writing—not an analytic abstract. Of course, it would be patently absurd to suggest that the bass line (shown in ex. 9.12) is what Webern thought lay behind what he was hearing. It is no more than a purely analytic symbol and distillation of the harmonic processes at work, not a substitute for them. On the other hand, it is precisely this kind of symbolic process that led Beethoven to the unique way he opens the variations in the last movement of the "Eroica": distilling out of the old *Prometheus* theme its harmonic bass line; offering the skeleton first, then gradually putting melodic-harmonic flesh on the bare bones. What it does show clearly is the combination of new and old harmonic progressions, incorporating—as though they were perfectly compatible—the circularity of m3 chromatic sets, the powerful Neapolitan cadential function, and the equally powerful, if not more so, dominant function. The return to F at the end, suggestive of harmonic closure, is certainly purposeful. Clearly,

Webern gained a renewed vision of tonal possibilities—something he had set aside earlier—largely, I believe, through his experience with symmetrical chromaticism. It was on the basis of these new understandings that he raised himself to the status of a master of harmony.

A closer look at Webern's root line discloses that wherever a m3 progression between two roots occurs, we find a symmetrical fifth, and wherever a dominant-tonic progression is identified, we find an asymmetrical fifth. Therefore, if we take the first four pitches of the root line—F/B; B♭/E♭— we see a symmetrical fifth followed by an asymmetrical fifth. This pattern of alternation remains consistent for the remainder of the root line: F/B; B♭/E♭; E♭/A; A/D; D/G♯; G♯/C♯; C♯/G; F♯/B. Is it purely coincidence that Webern seems to base this variation on a circle of fifths, albeit alternating perfect and diminished forms? We will explore this new circle and its implications in the next and final chapter.

Chapter Ten

A New Circle of Fifths

The Symbolic Nature of the Two Fifths

The great tensions produced by the dynamic opposition of asymmetry and symmetry are best expressed by two opposing fifths, each crucial to its domain: first, the asymmetrical fifth (perfect fifth), which stands for diatonic tonality, and, second, the symmetrical fifth (or augmented fourth/ diminished fifth tritone, the "diabolus in musica" of medieval theory), which stands for chromaticism organized by the equidistant divisions of the octave. These two fifths point symbolically not only to past music theory and practice but also to present and potentially future theory and practice.

The structures of these respective fifths (six semitones versus seven) are *crucially* different from each other—even as to how they relate to the need for the cadence. The half-step between them divides worlds of music history and thinking. For a time, these worlds—the tonal and the atonal—seemed totally irreconcilable. Now we know that they are seemingly opposite worlds bound together in the larger relationship of polarity, which contains their opposing tensions in the magnetic form of attraction-repulsion—forces long known to operate in nature and now beginning to be recognized as operative in music.

The fifth of seven semitones points to the diatonic step degrees in the major and minor scales. Both scales are asymmetrical. Six points to the chromatic hexachord, symmetrically organized, of twelve-tone practice. It also points to the whole tone scale, a particular and special instance of hexachordal structure that is built up on diatonic steps but is chromatic. Six also refers to the Guidonian hexachord of medieval practice, which is modal rather than tonal, and is itself symmetrical. With the addition of a whole seventh tone, the Guidonian hexachord, along with the other modes, leads ultimately to the asymmetry of the major-minor diatonic system.

Asymmetry—in order to articulate its open-endedness and ongoingness—had to develop the harmonic cadence, which characterizes tonal thinking at literally every turn of the phrase: the half close (I–V); the full close (V–I, IV–V–I, ii–V–I); the deceptive cadence (V–vi in a major key, V–VI in a minor key)—distinctions of the greatest importance as chromaticism increased. All this was necessary in order to provide for melodic, harmonic, rhythmic, and structural articulation.

The way to noncadencing symmetry was prepared at least two generations before atonality sprang on an unsuspecting world—prepared by the
seamless, endless phrases of Wagner's "floating" tonality and the enormous
expansions of phrase length characteristic of Bruckner and Mahler around
the turn of the century. With the loss of key-centeredness came the loss
of the cadence. No such thing was necessary or even possible any longer.
Chromatic symmetry, whether of the circular harmonic set of tonal practice or of the mirroring hexachord of twelve-tone practice, is as essentially
antithetic to the cadence as is atonality generally.

The asymmetrical fifth points to two primary tonal structural functions:
first, as dominant (V) to tonic (I) in tonally centered diatonicism; second,
as the basis for the great circle of fifths, which brings the whole tonal system of twenty-four major and minor keys into a *relational* symmetry. In that
system, chromaticism is tightly controlled and plays a largely dependent,
albeit very important, role. Its only real freedom lies in the multidirectionality made possible by altered chords. But at the same time, that freedom
can be curtailed at any moment by reasserting the hierarchic functions of
the diatonic steps.

The symmetrical fifth points completely away from V–I relations, or any
circle of fifths motions based on the asymmetrical fifth. It points away from
open-endedness to self-enclosure; away from freely expanding motion—
melodic or harmonic—to rotation and circularity; away from the asymmetrical ordering of diatonic steps with their mixtures to the limited catalog of
equidistant intervals that form symmetries based on the major second (0 2
4 6 8 10 12), the minor third (0 3 6 9 12), and the major third (0 4 8 12),
that is, respectively, the whole tone scale, the m3 circular harmonic set,
and the M3 harmonic set.

The New Circle of Fifths

Despite what looks like absolute incompatibility between these two symbolic fifths, it is possible to conjoin them so that they form new relationships similar to the old circle of fifths other than the basic one of movement
by asymmetrical fifths or crisscross ones that join equidistant intervals into
M3 and m3 relations. This new possibility points the way toward reconcil-
ing the asymmetrical and symmetrical, the tonal and atonal, and the diatonic and chromatic.

The circle of fifths allows only for motions based on adjacent positions,
that is, clockwise rising motions or counterclockwise falling motions: C–G–
D–A, etc.; C–F–B♭–E♭, etc. This relational circularity by fifth movement was
embodied musically in the bass of one of the most fundamental triadic,
diatonic harmonic progressions that grew out of Baroque practice, and it

continued well beyond into the nineteenth century. It is a progression that deployed all seven step degrees of the scale by fifth motion in the bass: I–IV–vii°–iii–vi–ii–V–I; or C–F–B(♮)–E–A–D–G–C. Inevitably, such deployment cannot avoid the symmetrical fifth that comes between IV and vii° in major and VI and ii° in minor. These diminished fifths are absorbed into the balancing asymmetrical fifth motions that dominate the respective progressions. It was an important aspect of J. S. Bach's harmonic vocabulary, and he taught it to his sons J. C. Bach and C. P. E. Bach, who in turn transmitted it by influence and example to Haydn and Mozart. One of the principal themes in Mozart's Symphony No. 1 (written when he was eight years old) is based on this harmonic progression, which is, in effect, a musical embodiment of a purely abstract theoretical rubric, the circle of fifths. In 1789, when he was 19, Beethoven composed two preludes "durch alle Dur-Tonarten," that is, "through all the major keys," which he thought well enough of in his more mature years to give a place in his catalog by designating them as Opus 39. Perhaps Opus 39 is not among Beethoven's best musical efforts, but it is certainly a tribute to his power already at an early age to encompass a large, abstract design musically, and it was important enough to him to make two attempts, not just one, to conquer the purely harmonic problem of moving through the keys as smoothly and convincingly as possible.

Contrasting with the asymmetrical fifth, which makes possible open, ongoing, consecutive motion through adjacent positions on the circle and not returning to the original position until the circle has been completed in either direction, the symmetrical fifth, by its very nature, is unable to do anything but rotate its constituent members, repeating itself ad infinitum. In short, it is completely closed up within itself: C→F♯ rotates its starting pitch to the next higher octave becoming C→F♯→C, or F♯→C rotates its starting pitch to form F♯→C→F♯. In either case there is no way to break out of the tritone or away from C or F♯. However, when the two fifths are mixed in successive patterns of alternating symmetry-asymmetry, two different arrangements of the old circle of fifths become possible. Each one disposes the adjacent positions differently but in identical alternating patterns of six and seven semitones. Pattern 1, starting from C, produces:

Figure 10.1. New Circle of Fifths, pattern 1.

Pattern 2, starting from F♯, that is, from the inversion of the initial interval of pattern 1, produces:

Figure 10.2. New Circle of Fifths, pattern 2.

While each pattern contains twelve pitches, neither pattern—unlike the old circle of fifths—rotates back to its initial pitch. What each can do, however, is continue the alternating six-seven semitone pattern by hooking onto the next pattern, from pattern 1 to pattern 2, or vice versa. Thus the only way to return to a starting position, say the C of pattern 1, is to go through the twelve pitches twice in two different arrangements. The same holds true, then, for F♯: you have to go through the twelve in two different orders before returning to F♯ again.

It is the tension between six and seven, or symmetry and asymmetry, that gives the pattern its tensility and symbolic power. Though hardly the same, if we were to translate the pattern from pitches to words, we could pair, for instance, atonal-tonal or chromatic-diatonic and still preserve the same degree of tensility and symbolic power.

There is at first no obvious way of using this new pattern in composition. But like the relational symmetry of the old circle of fifths, though with little or no practical *harmonic* value, these patterns produce their own (double-patterned) relational symmetry. Just as three-note or four-note chords of perfect fifths do not—except in the rarest tonal instances—constitute harmony in the usual sense, so dissonant chromatic chords built up of only pairs of consecutive symmetrical and asymmetrical fifths have extremely limited harmonic value. C–F♯–C♯–G and F♯–C–G–C♯ are, in fact, transpositions of each other. All other four-note chords from patterns 1 and 2 cycles will contain identically constructed chords, for example, C♯–G–D–A♭, E♭–A–E♮–B♭, G–C♯–A♭–D, and A–E♭–B♭–E♮. A small adjustment in the order of any of these chords will produce two consecutive pairs of perfect or asymmetrical fifths a tritone apart: C/G–F♯/C♯; G/D–C♯/G♯; etc. Such groupings of pitches form the basis for the "Petrouchka chord," which will pop up every time two perfect fifths or two major triads a tritone apart appear. While the old circle of fifths has more than symbolic value in diatonic tonality, representing as it does motion from key to key by dominant function, that doesn't seem to apply to the new patterns. Nevertheless, the symbolic value of the new interlocking patterns remains high.

The Nature of Polarity

Central to our discussion of symmetry and asymmetry in music is an understanding of the concept of polarity. For greater ease, directness, and clarity in trying to explain the nature of polarity, I am borrowing the symbol >—<, devised by Samuel Taylor Coleridge, which he "habitually employed," according to Owen Barfield, "in his notebooks, marginal annotations and some of his letters to friends . . . to avoid the tedium of writing out in full some phrase as 'is polarically related to' or 'is the polar opposite of.'"[1] The symbol >—< denotes a state of interrelationship between polar opposites that is living and dynamic; it is expressive of energies of opposite tendency, yet bound together in or toward the creation of something of which they are both constituent elements. Refracting Coleridge's thoughts on polarity through his own understanding, Barfield makes a very important distinction:

> Polarity is dynamic, not abstract. It is not a "mere balance or compromise," but a "living and generative interpenetration." Where logical opposites are contradictory, polar opposites are generative of each other—and together generative of new product. Polar opposites exist by virtue of each other *as well as* at the expense of each other; "each is that which it is called, relatively, by predominance of the one character or quality, not by the absolute exclusion of the other." Moreover, each quality or character is present *in* the other. We can and must distinguish, but there is no possibility of *dividing* them.[2]

The subtlety of Coleridge's thought does not make it easy to penetrate the nature of polarity. But Barfield's phrase, "polar opposites are generative of each other—and together generative of new product," and Coleridge's amplification, "each [polar opposite] is that which it is called, relatively, by predominance of the one character or quality, not by the absolute exclusion of the other," take us to the threshold of three interrelated polarities that symbolize music as it exists and, I believe, how it will develop: tonal >—< atonal, diatonicism >—< chromaticism, and asymmetry >—< symmetry. These polarities can be reversed—atonal >—< tonal, chromaticism >—< diatonicism, and symmetry >—< asymmetry. Stated the first way, tonal >—< atonal, etc., the three not-quite-but-almost synonymous terms tonal, diatonicism, and asymmetry suggest a chronological approach from the linear, historical side of the eighteenth century. Their interpenetration with the opposite trio of almost synonymous terms, atonal, chromaticism, and symmetry, represents the twentieth-century outcome of the two-century-long evolutionary process. When taken by itself, the reverse set of polarities, atonal >—< tonal, etc., stands as symbolic representation of the present state of early twenty-first-century music.

Whichever approach we take, whichever set of polarities we start from, it becomes clear that these pairs of polar opposites, understood quite apart from chronology, contain the fundamental conditions, symbolically stated, of what composers have had to deal with in the past, have to deal with today, and will undoubtedly continue to have to deal with in the future—that is, provided music continues to be composed with twelve discrete pitches. For example, although tonality in the first three decades of the nineteenth century was primarily based on the asymmetries of diatonicism, through the imaginative expansions and forays of Beethoven and Schubert chromatic symmetry began to make its first appearances both with respect to thematic-structural layout (e.g., the "Waldstein") and to harmonic circularity (more with Schubert than Beethoven). About a century later, at the peak of the development of twelve-tone composition—almost exclusively symmetrical—unmistakable signs of old diatonic-tonal harmonic progressions begin to make *their* surprise appearance (particularly in Schoenberg's Opuses 45 and 50b). First, symmetry interpenetrated asymmetry; then, the reverse.

Polarity and Asymmetry >——< Symmetry

Each polar opposite posits the other. One cannot exist without the other. Each resists the other. Inherent in each is the tendency to be only itself—never the other. Yet the tendency to resistance lies not so much in the innate character of the one as in the character of the other, for what each resists lies not in itself but in the other.

The transformation of an asymmetrical order into a symmetrical one and vice versa is more than a mechanical rearrangement of elements. It is a redistribution of the energies and tensions that produce one kind of structure and its contrary, yet complementary, opposite. Only at points of momentary rest is one or the other a particular form of those energies and tensions.

However, it is necessary to distinguish the effects on music of each. Because it is open-ended, asymmetry allows for a constantly self-renewing, ongoing stream of energy that would descend into unorganized musical babbling were it not for the structural articulations provided by cadences and the formal divisions they make possible, inseparably interfused with the release and articulation of physical energy made manifest in metric pulsation and rhythmic phraseology.

Symmetry, on the other hand, with its powerful urge toward self-enclosure, virtually seals itself off from all streams of goal-directed energy, seeking equilibrium instead, embodying itself in tightly packed structures that eschew cadence or other defining structural division. This explains, at least in part, why symmetrical rotation leads to compression and abbreviation—witness Webern—of all kinds, melodic, harmonic, rhythmic, and formal.

Total symmetry leads to frozen, self-enclosed forms. Asymmetry suggests the vitality of the life principle that needs the discipline of art, taste, and judgment; symmetry suggests the life principle hemmed in on all sides by its very perfection. The pressure of centripetal force, that is, toward compression, creates the tight, circular pattern of the symmetrical. It is a movement inward—toward a core, a center. The pressure of centrifugal force, that is, toward outward expansion, creates the freer, more open, noncircular pattern of the asymmetrical.

Altogether, there is a lovely paradox in the combination of these two images. Tonality, which is key-centered, is chiefly asymmetrical, that is, centrifugal. All motion is out from the center; tonality has a secure core, and it is therefore free to expand outward. Atonality has no key, and it therefore lacks a center. Because it has no core, no center, it *seeks* one, and thus it lends itself readily to symmetry, to the centripetal.

A major shift of energies or tensions in one pattern or configuration will produce the other. That is, it will compress the centrifugal to the centripetal and expand the centripetal to the centrifugal. The reason for asymmetry is the same as the reason for symmetry: each state of tensions and energies has a *particular* function to be realized. It is possible to imagine a large symmetrical structure that enfolds asymmetrical functions, as it is possible to imagine a large asymmetrical structure that enfolds symmetrical functions. Similarly, it is possible to conceive of either one transforming itself into the other, metaphorically turning itself inside out or outside in.

The morphological development of Western music is the history of the dynamic tensions existing between the polar opposites. Seen that way, it is easier to understand its transformations: of modality into tonality; of diatonicism into chromaticism; and of tonality into atonality. All these transformations were gradual. They were prepared and developed within the framework of what was to be transformed. It is only the habit of not looking deep below the surface of things that makes it appear as if the change from one "style" to another was not only outer directed, but also sudden, abrupt.

The equalization of the modes via musica ficta into the major-minor standardization took centuries. The tendency to think symmetrically in the twentieth century was nurtured for approximately one hundred years in nineteenth-century tonal music. We can now see with absolute clarity that all the stages in the development of Western music are the end result of preoccupation—however unconscious—with either asymmetry or symmetry and their intermixtures. Seeing this will help to prepare for the next major step, which theoretically will play with juxtapositions of asymmetry and symmetry and their intermixtures (asymmetry enfolding symmetry; symmetry enfolding asymmetry); it is the next great turn in the spiral of morphological change and will make manifest heightened musical consciousness, itself a form of spiritual development.

At the beginning of the twenty-first century we are aware that enormous changes lie ahead, many of them fraught with grave danger. In the area of culture, change will rule no less than in all other areas of human existence. It is quite impossible to predict what directions music will take, what it will sound like. Nonetheless, I have confidence that what I have demonstrated in this volume (the polarities of diatonicism >—< chromaticism, tonality >—< atonality, and asymmetry >—< symmetry) will continue to be the frame of the very broad field within which composers will seek to express themselves as artists. The vastness of these possibilities is just beginning to be glimpsed. It will take generations to master them. For all that we place such naive trust in what we call "history," and generously delude ourselves into believing that if we know the past, the future will be less opaque, no one, for example, in C. P. E. Bach's time, including Haydn himself, could have predicted a Beethoven, nor could anyone in the generation of Wagner and Brahms have predicted a Schoenberg, or atonality and serialism. As always, in the great periods of striving for mastery of means, art is and will continue to be made against uncertainty. Precisely because there is a waywardness and randomness to human existence, music as art—to be able to survive its own day and those to follow—must be made with an intensity and seriousness of purpose that overrides uncertainty. The impossible paradox of it all is embodied in Blake's epigram, "Eternity is in love with the productions of time." Every piece of ephemera that somehow miraculously survives is touched by Blake's visionary eternity.

Afterword

Polarity, Unity of Opposites, Contraries, Gyres

Throughout this book I have talked about the centuries-long struggle for predominance between chromaticism and diatonicism and the parallel struggle between symmetry and asymmetry. To ground this reflection of polar opposites in the art of music, I will show here how the elusive nature of polarity itself is refracted through the long-standing traditions of philosophy and how the powerful, resonating overtones of polar opposites are revealed in the minds of some of the greatest poets in the English language—Blake, Coleridge, and Yeats.

What emerges is a fascinating pattern or weave of ideas that, though seemingly "new" in the contexts in which they arise—perhaps because of the language or metaphors in which they are cast—turn out to be, in fact, quite "ancient," as Western thought goes. Indeed, these ideas, discoverable in the pre-Socratic dawn of Western civilization, have consistently appeared, in one form or another, century after century, taking on ever-fresh meaning while adapting themselves to the needs and understanding of the times.

The idea of polarity turns out to be universal in Western culture. It is a way of trying to grasp the meaning of the mystery of forces that seem to rule human destiny and nature. This more than justifies one more effort to show music—the most fluid and expressive of human arts—to be the perfect medium for reflecting in sound those polar energies.

The Heraclitean Fire and the Unity of Opposites

Heraclitus was famous in antiquity "for his doctrine that everything is in a state of flux."[1] A mystic, Heraclitus "regarded fire as the fundamental substance; everything, like flame in a fire, is born by the death of something else."[2] It is not difficult to move from the Heraclitean idea of perpetual flux to "another doctrine on which," according to Bertrand Russell, "he set even more store. . . . This was the doctrine of the mingling of opposites. 'Men do not know,' he says, 'how what is at variance agrees with itself. It is an attunement of opposite tensions, like that of the bow and the lyre.'"[3]

The pressure of the bow on the taut string of an instrument produces the friction that sets the strings vibrating, and this vibration produces the sound—a harmony of overtones and a unity resulting from "an attunement of opposite tensions." The unity that exists in the world is formed, according to Heraclitus, by the combination of opposites: "Mortals are immortals, and immortals are mortals, the one living the other's death and dying the other's life."[4]

"'War,' says Heraclitus, 'is the father of all and the king of all.'"[5] And again: "We must know that war is common to all and strife is justice, and that all things come into being and pass away through strife."[6] Heraclitean strife is connected with the "mingling of opposites"; opposites strive against and with each other to combine in harmony. Heraclitus: "Couples are things whole and things not whole, what is drawn together and what is drawn asunder, the harmonious and the discordant."[7]

Implicit in the metaphysics of Heraclitus is the concept of cosmic justice, "which prevents the strife of opposites from ever issuing in the complete victory of either," according to Russell.[8] In support of his statement, Russell quotes Heraclitus: "Fire lives the death of air, and air lives the death of fire; water lives the death of earth, earth that of water."[9]

Blake and the Moral Dimensions of the Contraries

William Blake's most immediately approachable symbol is his famous "contraries"—on a first level, polar opposites in the spirit of Coleridge's sign >—<. But, as we learn from Kathleen Raine's admirable study of the eclectic sources on which Blake drew, there is a far deeper level that, at the same time, incorporates the first. In his spiritually charged imagery and language, Blake's contraries carry the heavenly and earthly freight of an endless, unresolvable human and cosmic moral drama. Raine traces Blake's concept of contraries to the writings of Jacob Boehme, who taught the "doctrine of the one root from which spring the contraries"[10]—the doctrine of the unity of opposites. For Blake, "the contraries are not, as for the practicing alchemists, natural principles simply considered; they are, explicitly, good and evil, heaven and hell."[11] Boehme also taught that God the Father "is the eternal fire"[12]—more than casually reminiscent of Heraclitus's idea of fire as the fundamental universal substance. Raine says, "It is . . . on the authority of Boehme that Blake dares to affirm that the Jehovah of the Bible is 'no other than he who dwells in flaming fire.'"[13]

That Blake knew Boehme *and* Heraclitus is a certainty. For, as Raine says, "Blake . . . had access to the root of all such thought—the philosophy of Heraclitus and Empedocles—through the writings of Fludd (*Mosaicall Philosophy*). Fludd quotes Heraclitus as saying 'that all things were composed of strife and friendship; and Empedocles, that the soul was made of amity and enmity.' . . . Fludd's exposition of the cabala is full of this duality reconciled in unity."[14]

"It is from passages like these," Raine claims, "that Blake derived such thoughts as: 'Without Contraries is no progression' . . . and 'Attraction and Repulsion, Reason and Energy, Love and Hate, are necessary to human existence.'"[15] Blake, who was a voracious reader, was familiar with the thought of the Pythagoreans and Platonists and from them gathered ideas of the unity of opposites: "that all things were alive and in motion: they supposed a concord and discord, union and disunion, in particles, some attracting, others repelling each other . . . for the conservation and benefit of the whole."[16] Plotinus's *On Providence*, according to Raine, "states at length a similar view, that 'both good and evil are led through contraries in a beautiful order.'"[17]

The logical opposite of the contraries for Blake was negation. Negation destroyed the unity of opposite states by projecting a state of nonbeing that, to Blake, was utterly false and hateful. In *Milton*, he writes:

> There is a Negation, & there is a Contrary
> The Negation must be destroyd to redeem the Contraries
> The Negation is the Spectre; the Reasoning Power in Man:
> This is a false Body; an Incrustation over my Immortal
> Spirit; a Selfhood, which must be put off & annihilated alway[18]

Raine follows these lines with the comments that "the contraries—'married' by Blake in his heaven and hell—are good and evil, equally necessary to the progression of things," whereas "the difference between the contraries and the negation is that the former have essential existence, and the latter not."[19]

Music and the Moral Dimensions of Polarity

The question of the moral value of music is a long-standing one, not only in the West but also in Asia. Arthur Waley in his annotated translation of Confucius's *Analects* points out that Confucius saw in music something far more than pleasant sound or diversion from or accompaniment to cultured living. One of the analects of Confucius says: "Music, music! Does it mean no more than bells and drums?"[20] The "more" that sounds through the bells and drums is a moral presence—as active in the aesthetic realm as in any other human realm. This understanding is confirmed by Waley in his introduction to the *Analects* where he takes up the question of the indelible relationship between music and moral presence. There he tells the story of the Duke P'ing of Chin (placed by legend at around 533 BC) and what Waley calls "the baleful music"—music that projects evil, destructive forces: "drawn by the magic of an evil tune eight huge black birds swooped from the south and danced on his terrace, black clouds blotted out the sky, a tempest tore down the hangings of his palace, broke the ritual vessels, hurled down the tiles from the roof; the king fell sick, and for three years no blade of grass grew in Chin, no tree bore fruit."[21] According to Waley, Confucius asks his question "does music mean no more than bells and drums?" because music is far more than mere physical sound: music can be a powerful means for good, for the moral education of the characters of those who govern the state. Music has magical powers to move nature and man as well as the capacity to develop moral virtue in a just and orderly society. (Here we have the strongest possible pre-echo of the moral outcome of the strife of the polar opposites in *The Magic Flute.*)

The questions of the moral nature of music, its place in the social order, and its relation to the musical languages used are ancient and perennial, whether in the East or the West. As with all moral issues it is impossible to make precise statements of value, certainly not quantitative ones. It is possible, however, to say that when the moral values of music (and art generally) are tethered to ideologies such as socialist realism, political correctness, multiculturalism, and all such ideologies that attempt to exert control over those who make art or think about it, we may expect things to go wrong—and seriously so—because everything is stood on its head, and aggressive willfulness rules the day. Even as great an artist as Shostakovich could not transform into a positive the rule of socialist realism, an ideology that he overcame by the sheer force of his creative personality and tenacity of spirit.

The Sources of Coleridge's Polar Logic

In chapter 9 of his *Biographia Literaria* Coleridge claims "the polar logic and dynamic philosophy of Giordano Bruno" as the source of his ideas about polarity.[22] Owen Barfield, baffled by his inability to trace to any specific source in Bruno the concept of polarity *qua* polarity, nevertheless affirms Coleridge's claim when he says, "We know that he associated the universal law of polarity, as he understood it, especially with Bruno."[23]

In trying to track down the emergence of the concept of polarity in order to find a possible connection to Bruno, Barfield brings up the potentially related "coincidentia oppositorum"—the coincidence of opposites—an idea said to have originated with Nicolas of Cusa. Cusa's approach being primarily mathematical, Barfield concludes that "the 'feel' of Cusa's coincidence of opposites is that of a static relation between finity and infinity rather than of any energizing relation between infinitely expanding and infinitely contracting 'forces.'"[24] Barfield rejects any relationship between

the coincidence of opposites and polarity, concluding that "a logical contra-
diction such as coincidentia oppositorum is mere negation; contemplated
as 'paradox' it becomes, in a sense, affirmative and positive; but it is still
static. But the essence of polarity is a dynamic conflict between coinciding
opposites. Coleridge . . . cites Heraclitus as the first promulgator of the law
of polarity; and the element of conflict, the quality of psychic oppugnancy
between opposites is evident there in a way it hardly is in Bruno."[25] Quot-
ing Coleridge, Barfield offers in explanation of "oppugnancy," "two opposite and counteracting forces." Further, Barfield says: "We have seen also
that it is characteristic of the relation of polarity that although one pole,
one force cannot be without the other, yet there is always a predominance
of one over the other; further, that it is upon these varying and alternating
predominances that all evolution, and indeed life itself depends."[26]

Yeats and Gyres

The passionate preoccupation with the idea of the unity of opposites seen
as dynamic conflict and interaction takes on still another form—this time
more overtly mystical, even occult—with the thought of the poet William
Butler Yeats. He is far less interested in the purely philosophical, abstract
aspects of opposites than in the processes by which opposites, as states of
mind and soul, combine and recombine to produce the infinite variety of
human personality types as well as to affect individual destiny, and even the
destinies of entire cultures and societies. To this end, in *A Vision*, a book
written before World War II, he develops, with the guidance of "beings" he
calls his "instructors," a grand system of "Faculties" and "Principles" that
combine in virtually endless configurations of conflicting opposites struggling toward resolution of their frictions in a harmony of being. Yeats says
as much when he describes what he takes to be the purpose of his instructors: "My instructors identify consciousness with conflict, not with knowledge, substitute for subject and object and their attendant logic a struggle
towards harmony, towards Unity of Being. Logical and emotional conflict
alike lead towards a reality which is concrete, sensuous, bodily."[27]

These "Faculties" and "Principles," locked in strife, Yeats calls *gyres*,
which take the abstract form of geometric cones (see Yeats's diagrams in
part 1 of book 1 of *A Vision*, "The Great Wheel") that exist in a dynamic
state of constant interrelation and interpenetration striving for predominance over one another. "Gyres," Yeats says, "are occasionally alluded to,
but left unexplored, in Swedenborg's mystical writings. In the *Principia*, a
vast scientific work written before his mystical life, he describes the double
cone . . . where there are 'two poles, one opposite to the other, these two
poles have the form of cones.'"[28]

Yeats equates time with subjectivity—by which I assume he means the experience of duration, whereas "all that we can touch or handle," as he says, "has shape and magnitude"[29]—by which he must surely mean the experience of space. Thus he equates pure time with pure subjectivity and pure space with pure objectivity, calling pure time and pure space "abstractions or figments of the mind."[30] He reports: "My instructors . . . [preferred] to consider subjectivity and objectivity as intersecting states struggling one against the other."[31] He also tells us that his "mind had been full of Blake from boyhood up and I saw the world as a conflict— Spectre and Emanation—and could distinguish between a contrary and a negation. 'Contraries are positive,' wrote Blake, 'a negation is not a contrary.'"[32]

Yeats, in describing the elements of his system, says of the pairs of "Faculties" he sets up: "These pairs of opposites whirl in contrary directions,"[33] that is, clockwise and counterclockwise. These opposites are Yeats's gyres, which he traces back to Empedocles, the pre-Socratic philosopher and contemporary of Parmenides, in order to establish the core idea of gyres:

> "When Discord," writes Empedocles, "has fallen into the lowest depths of the vortex"—the extreme bound, not the centre, Burnet points out—"Concord has reached the centre, into it do all things come together so as to be only one, not all at once but gradually from different quarters, and as they come Discord retires to the extreme boundary . . . in proportion as it runs out Concord in a soft immortal boundless stream runs in." And again: "Never will boundless time be emptied of that pair; and they prevail in turn as that circle comes round, and pass away before one another and increase their appointed turn." It was this Discord or War that Heraclitus called "God of all and Father of all, some it has made gods and some men, some bond and some free," and I recall that Love and War came from the eggs of Leda.[34]

Yeats describes the cones or gyres of Discord and Concord as increasing or diminishing in opposite motions: "I see that the gyre of 'Concord' diminishes as that of 'Discord' increases, and can imagine after that the gyre of 'Concord' increasing while that of 'Discord' diminishes, and so on, one gyre within the other always. Here the thought of Heraclitus dominates all: 'Dying each other's life, living each other's death.'"[35]

Music and the Unity of Opposites

Whereas in metaphysics and mysticism the unity and reconciliation of opposites remains an ideal, in the art of music we find its concrete embodiment. What has largely escaped human beings in their social, economic,

and political lives—the ability to achieve harmony and balance among contending forces—has found its finest realization in music.

Long-established habits of routine theoretical and scholarly thinking
have dulled understanding of the opposing energies that have shaped
Western music virtually from its beginning. To help restore the vital mem-
ory of these polar opposites with which composers have been working in
increasingly complex forms, I will discuss briefly those I consider absolutely fundamental because they are, as Yeats says, "concrete, sensuous,
bodily" forms of the strife and tensions produced by opposite forces. These
are—not necessarily in order of importance—contrary motion, as we find
it in species counterpoint; dissonance-consonance resolutions in the development of harmony; the pitting of slow against fast whether understood
as contrapuntal subject and countersubject (or counterpoint), or different speeds contending against each other in the same music, or different
tempi in the same music in direct opposition to each other; and metric
subdivision of a large, slow beat and resulting centripetal intensification.

By the time of Johann Joseph Fux's *Gradus ad Parnassum* (1725), a theoretical work much admired by musicians of the eighteenth century, contrapuntal motion between two or more parts had been codified into three
categories: contrary, direct, and oblique. Contrary motion between voices
(or parts) was acknowledged as the strongest possible motion, because
it produces the most active tensions. Direct motion was considered the
weakest and least interesting because it negated tension; oblique motion
retained tension, since it allowed one voice or part to move toward or away
from a single, static note or part. These motions were mixed, of course—
especially once counterpoints of two to four notes against each note of the
moving cantus firmus (literally: fixed song) came into play.

The history of counterpoint precedes the history of harmony by about
five hundred years. Harmony *qua* harmony grew slowly out of the rhythmic
practices of contrapuntal music. Harmonic "concord" or "discord" had to
be taken into account as the individual parts came together to form a total
texture. A harmonic vocabulary was gradually established as the language
of tonality. Incorporated into this language were the devices of moving
parts, which evolved from the practices of counterpoint: dissonant intervals
of suspension resolving to consonant intervals of resolution. Again, tension
is produced through opposites. Thus 9→8, 7→6, 4→3 resolutions, which
had their roots in contrapuntal practice, continued to function in harmonic practice. They incorporated the tensions of opposite states of aural
perception—dissonance and consonance—into a context that sought the
ultimate reconciliation of all tension-producing forces, whether of sound
or motion.

The principle of the resolution of dissonance into consonance developed the harmonic language of tonality, the most fundamental functional

harmonic dissonance being, of course, the dominant seventh chord, which demanded resolution to its tonic. One could even assign to this principle the contrasting opposition of major and minor modes in same-key tonalities. (Schubert, Brahms, and Mahler made much of this device.) Once transformation through chromatic symmetry had radically altered the character of music, dissonant harmonies *without* resolutions came to be the rule, existing in their own right and independent of traditional tonal functions of dissonance-consonance, or tension-resolution. But dissonant harmony—whether in the manner of Scriabin or Debussy or Ravel—tended to produce a homogeneity of sound in which pitch conflict or tension became weakened and tended to disappear. The effect of such music— whether considered mystical, impressionistic, or symbolist—was pastel, silkenly sensuous, tensionless. In the final stage of transformation into atonal, twelve-tone, and serial pitch worlds, dissonant intervals and dissonant harmonic compounds were intensified to a high degree of aural and psychological tension bordering on the physically exhausting. But as these forms of chromaticism disavowed consonance resolutions as a matter of principle, another kind of sameness developed, this time unrelieved in its effect of harsh, expressionistic, sharply acerbic, hard, sometimes metallic, often fragmented surfaces.

Here we have almost a pure case of Blake's negation at work canceling out contraries: opposites—dissonance >——< consonance—destroyed by negation, in this particular case, by the negation of consonance. One can also imagine an entirely *consonant* music that destroys *its* contrary by the negation of dissonance. Where one or the other of contraries wins out, no unity of opposites is possible. Though the war has ceased, it cannot be said that peace has been established—unless we mean the false peace of tyranny and oppression. Both kinds of homogeneity brought about by the utter suppression of the opposite—in both these twentieth-century instances the opposite being consonance—produced short-lived "styles" of music-making. The return of the tonal possibility in the 1970s and 1980s ensured the reestablishment of the principle of opposites, their conflicting struggle, and possible unity through resolution.

By extending the principle of species counterpoint that sets two or more notes against each note of the cantus firmus, we can establish an opposition through two speeds: slow against fast. What is more, we can extend the idea of a slow-moving part contending against a fast- (or faster-) moving part to the idea of different *musics* moving against each other, thus intensifying the idea of absolute opposites—different musics meaning, of course, ones based on opposite speeds, gestures, and pitch worlds—making a kind of virtual combat between hostile, alien musics. Carried too far, of course, such "combat" scenarios quickly degenerate into noise, aural chaos. It may "save the appearance" of such an aesthetic to call it a mirror reflection of the world as it *really* is, but I see no virtue in merely replicating the crass and the obvious. In that direction no artistic imagination is required. The absence of art is hardly the same as hiding art.

The various forms of extension of contrapuntal practice are readily illustrated. In the chorale preludes of J. S. Bach—his own large repertoire the climax of a long tradition among German Protestant composers—we find the opposition of the phrases of a slow cantus firmus embedded in the faster-moving figurations of a beautifully designed independent texture of other parts, all controlled by Bach's profound sense of harmony. There is a fine continuation of the chorale prelude tradition in the knights' chorale in Mozart's *The Magic Flute* and a superb example in the "Heiliger Dankgesang" movement of Beethoven's String Quartet in A minor, Op. 132. But it is in the A$^\flat$ section of Beethoven's *Grosse Fuge*, Op. 133, starting at measure 273, that we find not only the opposition of slow against fast speeds raised to a new level of dramatic tension but also the seeds of the opposition of *different* musics planted for the first time (even though harmonic agreement among parts still prevails) in nineteenth-century music. Berlioz takes this tendency toward opposing speeds through different musics a step further in the remarkable fugue in the last movement of his *Symphonie fantastique.* Wagner makes his contribution to this new stream of opposing speeds and musics in his treatment of the "Pilgrims' Chorus" of *Tannhäuser.*

It is in the twentieth century with Charles Ives that the idea of *different* musics pitted in direct opposition to each other reaches full flower. There are two such Ivesian gems explicitly based on this opposition of speed, gestures, and pitch worlds: *The Unanswered Question,* in which Ives pits atonal, heavily dissonant chromatic phrases of short duration against a continuous diatonic background for strings in the key of G major; and *Central Park in the Dark,* in which the string orchestra repeats a heavily chromaticized quasi-impressionistic harmonic progression of ten measures, against which Ives introduces the blatant, vulgar ragtime of a popular tune of the day, "Hello, Ma Baby." Out of Ives's idea of colliding musics emerged the possibility of "collage music," in which different musics—including quotations—collide in a calculated, partially controlled chaos.

Finally, one more variety of the use of the opposites of slow against fast may be found in the slow movements of Haydn, Mozart, and Beethoven. In the examples I have in mind we find a slow beat subdivided into increasingly smaller durational values without changing the speed of the beat itself. This has the effect of compressing and intensifying—through the increased friction of slow $>\!\!-\!\!<$ fast values—the inner rhythmic movement of the music. A prime instance of such slow beat subdivision occurs in the Andante cantabile of Mozart's "Jupiter" Symphony. The basic beat is a quarter note. The subdivisions that Mozart employs are principally sixteenths and thirty-seconds. At measure 20 Mozart introduces sixteenth triplets, which produce a new urgency. This urgency is further intensified by the syncopated figure ♪ ♫♫♫♩ starting at measure 19 in the first violins, coupled with the syncopated figure ♫♫♫♩ of the second violins and violas against the steady eighth-note subdivision in cellos and basses. Against this combination of somewhat agitated, varied subdivisions the winds and horns play the slower values based on the quarter-note beat. A relative calm ensues at measure 28 with the enlargement of the earlier triplet sixteenth figure into a sextuplet sixteenth inner voice played by the second violins. At measure 32 the sextuplet takes over the melody in the first violins (and later, flute).

As he did with everything else he inherited directly from Haydn and Mozart, Beethoven developed slow-movement subdivision of the fundamental beat to a high art. I will simply mention here three of innumerable instances in his output: the "Marcia funebre" of the "Eroica," the Adagio of Symphony No. 4, and the "Arietta" variations of the last piano sonata, Opus 111. They illustrate the principle of compression that results from subdivided beats.

Brahms takes the classical device of centripetal compression through beat subdivision a step further when he fashions two metrically different versions of the trio, which provides animated contrast to the Allegretto grazioso of his Second Symphony. Here the trio is totally opposite in spirit to the Allegretto grazioso yet united to it by the fact that both versions of the trio are rapidly moving beat subdivisions of the Allegretto's quarter note main beat.

Music and the Contraries of the Human Soul

Music is real—as real as the human beings who make it. And it is because music is real, in fact, as crucial and serious as any other reality within the broad range of human experience, that we can declare it a direct expression, an uncompromised projection of the states of the human heart and soul. These states lead us directly into the condition of the human spirit as it lives and struggles with the forces and experiences that affect it.

That is why I believe it is possible to describe Mahler's Symphony No. 7 Scherzo as a music of terror, of dread, and of fearful anxiety; or to say the Adagio last movement of his Ninth Symphony is a desperately sad music of heartbreak, a music of "the night of the soul"; or to attribute to Beethoven's Seventh Symphony Scherzo and last movement a state of unparalleled release of ecstatic joyousness. All such musics are fully alive; that is, they take on a life apart from their composers. Were this not true, then neither could it be said to be true of Shakespeare's characters—Hamlet or Lear or Macbeth or Shylock—that they live in human consciousness perhaps even more powerfully than flesh-and-blood individuals. Through the magic of art, such music and such characters become real. And with that reality they enter into the human world of good and evil, heaven and hell, innocence and experience.

In the consensus that has raised Mozart to the exalted state of an angel of music, one work stands as the virtually perfect symbol of the conflict between the contraries, the opposites of good and evil, of light and dark forces: *The Magic Flute*. No more than it can be said that it was the Elizabethan language that made Shakespeare's characters live as they do can it be said that eighteenth-century tonality endowed *The Magic Flute*—or, for that matter, any of Mozart's music—with its purity of spiritual essence. Nor can it be said that Beethoven's *Fidelio* succeeds in celebrating the victory of the human spirit over tyranny and political oppression *because* it is tonal; nor that Wagner's *Götterdämmerung* stands as the symbol of world ruination through unrestrained evil *because* the massive weight of unrestricted chromaticism crushed tonality.

There has to be, of course, an appropriateness of fit between the composer and his means, between the musical language at his disposal and how he uses it. But the means, the language used, does not determine the spiritual outcome. It is the essence of the composer that leaves its imprint on the means through which he works.

In the same spirit of responding to music through its inner states I find it impossible to think of Schoenberg's *Pierrot Lunaire* without a strong visceral sense of the toxicity of its sickness of spirit; or to think of Bartók's *Miraculous Mandarin* without an equally strong sense of the corrosive acids of its expressionism. In neither case do I attribute the responses to moral deficiencies in their composers. If there is an explanation, I am convinced it lies in the direction of the supersensitivity of Schoenberg's and Bartók's spiritual antennae to the extraordinarily disturbed conditions of the real world around them. No one would dispute the sickness of soul, the malaise and general dispiritedness of pre–World War I Europe—the world of *Pierrot Lunaire*—or the evil, corrosive poisons of the destructive spirit of pre–World War II Europe produced by the witches' brew of Nazism, Fascism, and Communism—the world of *Miraculous Mandarin*. Here again, the fit of the works to the means employed depends entirely on the capacity of their composers to project their moral sense of a world gone wrong. That atonality and an intensely dissonant harmonic palette are, respectively, more appropriate to *Pierrot Lunaire* and *Miraculous Mandarin* than to eighteenth-century tonality is not surprising. Yet there are some curious anomalies: for example, Stravinsky's *Rake's Progress*, which is a highly personalized adaptation of the tonal language of the eighteenth century, a work depicting individual debauchery and spiritual ruin; and Schoenberg's *A Survivor from Warsaw*, which celebrates through its use of the twelve-tone method the victory of the human spirit over the monstrous evil that is the Holocaust. But then again the horrendous fate of the unregenerate Don Giovanni is projected by Mozart solely through eighteenth-century tonality, as the pathologically confused Wozzeck is cast by Alban Berg in twelve-tone terms.

Polar Opposites in Music: Qualities vs. Quantities

Polar opposites appear in music as qualities and are not reducible to formulaic, mechanistic terms. Even when we use numbers to designate intervallic and harmonic dissonance resolving to consonance (as in figured bass notation or various systems of analysis), we are trying to distinguish between opposite qualitative, that is, emotional or psychological, states, not quantitative states. The same is essentially true in applying metronomic numbers to the speed of beats, their opposition through difference or compression through subdivision: qualities of motion, of emotion, are being designated, not quantities. This distinction is crucial and goes a long way toward explaining why music is *not*—as some would have it—mathematics. In ancillary fashion it goes a very long way toward an understanding of why, even though science and technology almost completely dominate current human society, quantitative values and measurements, so essential to basic scientific thought, are totally inappropriate to the creation of art, especially the art of music. Despite misguided thinking in the twentieth-century avant-garde, they simply do not fit.

Science wants to understand—in theoretical and empirical terms—how the universe works. Technology wants to manipulate—for (presumably) human benefit—the physical environment. Art wants neither to prove anything nor to manipulate anything. Art wants to project an endless stream of individual, subjective experience by expressing that infinite, ever-changing variety of experience purely in qualitative terms. Art is not interested in proof or demonstration. If it were, it would not be art. That artistic expression employs syntactical or logical forms in order to project itself in clear, perceptible terms in no way compromises its essentially nonquantitative nature. To say that Renaissance painters used the grid to help them organize their visual representations or that poets have used lines of so many feet and devised complex end-rhyme schemes or that Baroque composers frequently wrote out melodic parts supported only by a figured basso continuo line in no way converts such practices into forms of science or technology.

Polar opposites in music are qualities brought into purposeful conflict, expressive friction and tension. As a result, it is possible to imagine a grand, morphological pas de deux—a dance of polar opposites—in which there are innumerable and subtle combinations of steps and fig-

ures, in which raw juxtapositions of tonality >—< atonality, diatonicism
>—< chromaticism, and asymmetry >—< symmetry produce sharp con-
trasts, in which asymmetry enfolds symmetry, symmetry enfolds asymmetry. It is the ongoing tensions between these qualitative forces, states, and
conditions that ensure the continuation of music as an art. It is its own
form of Heraclitus's flux, Blake's contraries, Coleridge's polar opposites,
Yeats's gyres, which have conveyed for millennia the same constant struggle for the unity and reconciliation of opposites.

Appendix One

George Rochberg Archives

Collections, American Academy of Arts and Letters, New York, NY (http://www.artsandletters.org/collections.php).

George Rochberg Collection, Paul Sacher Foundation, Basel, Switzerland (http://www.paul-sacher-stiftung.ch/en/home.html).

George Rochberg Music Room, John J. Cali Music Building, Montclair State University, Montclair, NJ (http://www.montclair.edu/index.php).

George Rochberg Papers, Music Division, The New York Public Library for the Performing Arts, New York, NY (http://www.nypl.org/locations/lpa).

Music Library and Rare Books Room, Van Pelt Library, University of Pennsylvania, Philadelphia, PA (http://www.library.upenn.edu/vanpelt/).

Performing Arts, Library of Congress, Washington, DC (http://www.loc.gov/index.html).

Rock Resource Center, Curtis Institute of Music, Philadelphia, PA (http://www.curtis.edu/about-curtis/facilities/rock-resource-center/).

Theodore Presser Company, King of Prussia, PA (http://www.presser.com/).

Appendix Two

Celebrating George Rochberg's Eightieth Year

1998 performances

Clarinet Concerto

Curtis Orchestra, Anthony Gigliotti, clarinet, Robert Spano conducting

March 1   Academy of Music, Philadelphia, PA

Circles of Fire for 2 pianos

Evan Hirsch — Sally Pinkas Duo

PREMIERE PERFORMANCES

March 6	Duke University, Durham, NC
March 31	University of Pennsylvania at Curtis Institute of Music, Philadelphia, PA
April 4	Hopkins Center, Dartmouth College, Hanover, NH
April 5	University of Vermont, Burlington, VT
May 2	Arizona State University, Tempe, AZ

Octet and Chamber Symphony

Orchestra 2001, James Freeman conducting

March 20	Lang Hall, Swarthmore College, Swarthmore, PA
March 22	Adademy of Vocal Arts, Philadelphia, PA

Eden: Out of Time and Out of Space, Chamber Concerto for Guitar and Six Players

Eliot Fisk, guitarist

PREMIERE PERFORMANCES

July 2 & 3	Chamber Music Pacific Northwest, Portland, OR
November 15 & 17	Chamber Music Society at Lincoln Center, Tully Hall, New York, NY

Black Sounds, Octet, Cantio Sacra, Phaedra for Soprano and Orchestra

Boston Modern Orchestra Project, Retrospective Concert, Gilbert Rose conducting

October 17   Boston, MA

Notes

Introduction

1. George Rochberg, *The Hexachord and Its Relation to the 12-Tone Row* (King of Prussia, PA: Theodore Presser Company, 1955), vii.

2. George Rochberg, *Five Lines, Four Spaces: The World of My Music*, ed. Gene Rochberg and Richard Griscom (Urbana: University of Illinois Press, 2009), 144.

3. The full text of *Chromaticism* is preserved in the George Rochberg Collection of the Paul Sacher Foundation in Basel, Switzerland.

4. Alan Gilmore, ed., *Eagle Minds: Selected Correspondence of Istvan Anhalt and George Rochberg* (Waterloo, Ontario, Canada: Wilfrid Laurier University Press, 2007), 272.

5. George Rochberg, *The Aesthetics of Survival: A Composer's View of Twentieth-Century Music*, rev. ed. (Ann Arbor: University of Michigan Press, 2004), 250.

6. "The Harmonic Tendency of the Hexachord," published 1959, and "Webern's Search for Harmonic Identity," published 1962, both in the *Journal of Music Theory*, as well as *The Hexachord and Its Relation to the 12-Tone Row*.

7. George Perle, review of *The Hexachord and Its Relation to the 12-Tone Row*, by George Rochberg, *Journal of American Musicological Society* 10, no. 1 (1957): 55–59. George Rochberg, review of *Serial Composition and Atonality*, by George Perle, *Journal of American Musicological Society* 16, no. 3 (1963): 413–18.

8. Richard Cohn, "Introduction to Neo-Riemannian Theory: A Survey and a Historical Perspective," *Journal of Music Theory* 42, no. 2 (1998): 168.

9. It occurs on page 507 of part 4.

10. Richard Taruskin, *Stravinsky and the Russian Traditions: A Biography of the Works through Mavra*, vol. 1 (Berkeley: University of California Press, 1996), 256.

Chapter Three

1. Arnold Schoenberg, *Style and Idea*, ed. Leonard Stein, trans. Leo Black (Berkeley: University of California Press, 1975), 263.

Chapter Five

1. Because the work is too long to give in its entirety, I urge the reader to follow the score as the analysis unfolds.

Chapter Nine

1. For Rochberg's analysis of the symmetries at work in Contrapuncti 12 and 13 see his appendix to *Circles of Fire for Two Pianos* (Theodore Presser Company, 2000, pp. 150–56).
2. Anton Webern, *The Path to the New Music*, ed. Willi Reich, trans. Leo Black (King of Prussia, PA: Theodore Presser Company, 1963), 28.
3. For Webern, the "tonal field" (*Tonbereich*) denoted the expanding pitch palette afforded composers, developing from modal to diatonic to chromatic resources. See lectures 3–6 from *The Path to the New Music*.
4. Webern, *The Path to the New Music*, 28–29, 36–39.

Chapter Ten

1. Owen Barfield, *What Coleridge Thought* (Middletown, CT: Wesleyan University Press, 1971), 35.
2. Barfield, *What Coleridge Thought*, 36.

Afterword

1. Bertrand Russell, *A History of Western Philosophy* (New York: Simon & Schuster, 1945), 41.
2. Russell, *A History of Western Philosophy*, 41.
3. Russell, *A History of Western Philosophy*, 43.
4. Russell, *A History of Western Philosophy*, 41.
5. Russell, *A History of Western Philosophy*, 41.
6. Russell, *A History of Western Philosophy*, 42.
7. Russell, *A History of Western Philosophy*, 44.
8. Russell, *A History of Western Philosophy*, 44.
9. Russell, *A History of Western Philosophy*, 44.
10. Kathleen Raine, *Blake and Tradition*, Bollingen Series 35.11, 2 vols. (Princeton: Princeton University Press, 1968), 1:361.
11. Raine, *Blake and Tradition*, 1:361.
12. Raine, *Blake and Tradition*, 1:361.
13. Raine, *Blake and Tradition*, 1:363.
14. Raine, *Blake and Tradition*, 1:426. I refer the interested reader to Raine's fulsome quotation from Fludd's *Mosaicall Philosophy*.
15. Raine, *Blake and Tradition*, 1:363.
16. Raine, *Blake and Tradition*, 1:363.
17. Raine, *Blake and Tradition*, 1:363–64.
18. David V. Erdman, ed., *The Complete Poetry and Prose of William Blake*, rev. ed. (New York: Anchor Books, 1988), 142.
19. Raine, *Blake and Tradition*, 2:220.
20. Arthur Waley, trans., *The Analects of Confucius*, book 17, no. 11 (New York: Vintage Books, 1938), 212.
21. Waley, *The Analects of Confucius*, 68.

22. Barfield, *What Coleridge Thought*, 179.

23. Barfield, *What Coleridge Thought*, 181.

24. Barfield, *What Coleridge Thought*, 186.

25. Barfield, *What Coleridge Thought*, 187.

26. Barfield, *What Coleridge Thought*, 89.

27. William Butler Yeats, *A Vision* (New York: Collier Books, Macmillan Publishing Co., 1937, 1938, 1965), 214.

28. Yeats, *A Vision*, 69.

29. Yeats, *A Vision*, 71.

30. Yeats, *A Vision*, 71.

31. Yeats, *A Vision*, 71.

32. Yeats, *A Vision*, 72.

33. Yeats, *A Vision*, 74.

34. Yeats, *A Vision*, 67.

35. Yeats, *A Vision*, 68.

Bibliography

Barfield, Owen. *What Coleridge Thought.* Middletown, CT: Wesleyan University Press, 1971.

Cohn, Richard. "Introduction to Neo-Riemannian Theory: A Survey and a Historical Perspective." *Journal of Music Theory* 42, no. 2 (1998): 167–80.

Erdman, David V., ed. *The Complete Poetry and Prose of William Blake.* Rev. ed. New York: Anchor Books, 1988.

Gilmore, Alan, ed. *Eagle Minds: Selected Correspondence of Istvan Anhalt and George Rochberg.* Waterloo, Ontario, Canada: Wilfrid Laurier University Press, 2007.

Laitz, Steven G. *The Complete Musician: An Integrated Approach to Tonal Theory, Analysis, and Listening.* New York, Oxford: Oxford University Press, 2008.

Perle, George. Review of *The Hexachord and Its Relation to the 12-Tone Row*, by George Rochberg. *Journal of American Musicological Society* 10, no. 1 (1957): 55–59.

Raine, Kathleen. *Blake and Tradition.* 2 vols. Bollingen Series 35.11. Princeton: Princeton University Press, 1968.

Rochberg, George. *Five Lines, Four Spaces: The World of My Music.* Edited by Gene Rochberg and Richard Griscom. Urbana: University of Illinois Press, 2009.

———. *The Aesthetics of Survival: A Composer's View of Twentieth-Century Music*, Rev. ed. Ann Arbor: University of Michigan Press, 2004.

———. "The Harmonic Tendency of the Hexachord." *Yale Journal of Music Theory* 3, no. 2 (1959): 208–30.

———. *The Hexachord and Its Relation to the 12-Tone Row.* King of Prussia, PA: Theodore Presser Company, 1955.

———. Review of *Serial Composition and Atonality*, by George Perle. *Journal of American Musicological Society* 16, no. 3 (1963): 413–18.

———. "Webern's Search for Harmonic Identity." *Yale Journal of Music Theory* 6, no. 1 (1962): 109–22.

Russell, Bertrand. *A History of Western Philosophy.* New York: Simon & Schuster, 1945.

Schoenberg, Arnold. *Style and Idea*, edited by Leonard Stein, translated by Leo Black. Berkeley: University of California Press, 1975.

Taruskin, Richard. *Stravinsky and the Russian Traditions: A Biography of the Works through Mavra.* Vol. 1. Berkeley: University of California Press, 1996.

Waley, Arthur, trans. *The Analects of Confucius.* New York: Vintage Books, 1938.

Webern, Anton. *The Path to the New Music*, edited by Willi Reich, translated by Leo Black. King of Prussia, PA: Theodore Presser Company, 1963.

Yeats, William Butler. *A Vision.* New York: Collier Books, Macmillan Publishing Co., 1937, 1938, 1965.

Index

In *A Dance of Polar Opposites: The Continuing Transformation of Our Musical Language*, the renowned American composer George Rochberg distilled a lifetime of insights about Western music across some three hundred years. Rochberg describes how the asymmetrical tonal language of the late eighteenth century—the era of Haydn and Mozart—evolved through the gradual incursion of symmetry into a system based on the juxtaposition of tonal and atonal, asymmetrical and symmetrical—as seen in notable composers such as Webern, Prokofiev, and Rochberg himself.

A Dance of Polar Opposites takes us inside the composer's studio, reveals how he assessed his and our musical past, and paints a picture of what he believed our musical future may be.

George Rochberg (1918–2005), one of the most respected composers and writers about music in the second half of the twentieth century, was a finalist twice for the Pulitzer Prize and longtime professor at University of Pennsylvania. His writings include *The Aesthetics of Survival: A Composer's View of Twentieth-Century Music* (which won the ASCAP-Deems Taylor Award); the memoir *Five Lines, Four Spaces*; and a volume of letters.

Jeremy Gill was a student of George Rochberg and is a composer, conductor, and pianist.

"With this unique and stunning work, Rochberg opens the door for readers to look freshly at both tonal and atonal music of the past. It includes passionate views on masterworks from Mozart to Webern and should be a must read for any composer, music student, or lover of our art."

—Norman Fischer, Herbert S. Autrey
Professor of Cello, Rice University, and
former cellist, Concord String Quartet

"The joy of reading George Rochberg's aesthetic writings is his breadth of vision—his ability to step outside of history and hear the unity of music beneath the warring dualisms others hear. In *A Dance of Polar Opposites*, he shows just how short the distance from Mozart to Stravinsky can be when we look at music as a dance of symmetries and asymmetries. It's a book to be read at the piano—the compelling musical examples bring to life what Rochberg hauntingly calls "the shadow of futurity."

—Kyle Gann, author of *No Such Thing as Silence: John Cage's 4'33"*